Managing for Health

This exciting new addition to the Routledge Studies in Health Management series concentrates on the management of the public health function and how it is different from the management of clinical work. The authors provide a unique comparative perspective on the issues of health improvement and the struggle between the needs of acute care providers such as hospitals and those that provide preventative measures to promote health. They posit the theory that unless the attempt is made to control the rising demand for health care services and redirect it to preventative measures all health care systems funded through public means will become unsustainable.

The key issues that the book addresses include:

- the concept of managing for health, or public health management
- the importance of public health management
- the skills and frameworks required of managers and practitioners working in health systems
- implications for training and development

Through examples and case studies drawn from across Europe the text explores the management challenge in public health policy and offers pointers to equip students of health management and public health managers with the necessary perspectives and skills to function effectively in the twenty-first century. Combining the very best of theory and practice *Managing for Health* will be essential reading for all those studying or working in this complex area.

David J. Hunter is Professor of Health Policy and Management, School for Health, Durham University where he heads up the Centre for Public Policy and Health. He is Chair of the UK Public Health Association. His research interests are in public health policy and implementation. He is author of *Public Health Policy* (Polity) and co-editor with Sian Griffiths of *New Perspectives in Public Health* (Radcliffe), now in its second edition.

ROUTLEDGE HEALTH MANAGEMENT SERIES

Edited by Marc Berg, Robbert Huijsman, David J. Hunter, John Øvretveit

Routledge Health Management is one of the first series of its kind, filling the need for a comprehensive and balanced series of textbooks on core management topics specifically oriented towards the health care field. In almost all Western countries, health care is seen to be in a state of radical reorientation. Each title in this series will focus on a core topic within health care management, and will concentrate explicitly on the knowledge and insights required to meet the challenges of being a health care manager. With a strong international orientation, each book draws heavily on case examples and vignettes to illustrate the theories at play. A genuinely groundbreaking new series in a much-needed area, this series has been put together by an international collection of expert editors and teachers.

Health Information Management
Integrating information and communication
Marc Berg with others

Health Operations Management
Patient flow logistics in health care
Edited by Jan Vissers and Roger Beech

Leadership in Health Care
A European perspective
Neil Goodwin

Performance Management in Health Care
Improving patient outcomes: an integrated approach
Edited by Jan Walburg, Helen Bevan, John Wilderspin and Karin Lemmens

Managing for Health
Edited by David J. Hunter

Managing for Health

Edited by

David J. Hunter

Routledge
Taylor & Francis Group

LONDON AND NEW YORK

First published 2007
by Routledge
2 Park Square, Milton Park, Abingdon, Oxon OX14 4RN

Simultaneously published in the USA and Canada
by Routledge
270 Madison Ave, New York, NY 10016

Routledge is an imprint of the Taylor & Francis Group, an Informa business

Typeset in Perpetua and Bell Gothic by
Florence Production Ltd, Stoodleigh, Devon
Printed and bound in Great Britain by
Antony Rowe Ltd, Chippenham, Wiltshire

British Library Cataloguing in Publication Data
A catalogue record for this book is available from the British Library

Library of Congress Cataloging in Publication Data
Managing for health/edited by David J. Hunter.
   p. cm.
   Includes bibliographical references and index.
     ISBN 0–415–36344–6 (hard cover) — ISBN 0–415–36345–4
   (soft cover) 1. Health services administration. 2. Public health
   administration. I. Hunter, David J.

RA393.M293 2007
362.1—dc22   2006028882

ISBN10: 0–415–36344–6 (hbk)
ISBN10: 0–415–36345–4 (pbk)
ISBN10: 0–203–01434–0 (ebk)

ISBN13: 978–0–415–36344–0 (hbk)
ISBN13: 978–0–415–36345–7 (pbk)
ISBN13: 978–0–203–01434–9 (ebk)

Contents

CONTENTS

Illustrations

FIGURES

TABLE

BOXES

LIST OF ILLUSTRATIONS

Contributors

THE EDITOR

David J. Hunter is Professor of Health Policy and Management in the School for Health, Wolfson Research Institute, Durham University. His research interests are in public health policy and practice and health policy and management, and he has published extensively in these areas. He has been Chair of the UK Public Health Association since April 2003.

OTHER CONTRIBUTORS

Kathryn Bailey is currently an Assistant Director at the North East Public Health Observatory, based at Durham University. She qualified as a primary school teacher at the University of Sunderland before joining the NHS in 1993 as an Information Officer. Her interest lies in making the best use of data and information to support public health policy and practice.

Mats Brommels, formerly co-director of the management programme at the Nordic School of Public Health, Gothenburg, Sweden, has presently a joint professorship in health services management at the University of Helsinki, Finland, and the Karolinska Institute, Stockholm, Sweden. He is also the director of the Medical Management Centre at the Karolinska Institute.

Catherine Hannaway is Network Programme Manager with the Association of Public Health Observatories. She was formerly Assistant Director Public Health and Performance Improvement, Yorkshire and the Humber NHS, UK. She is a former national programme director at the NHS Modernisation Agency. Having begun her career as a midwife, she is Programme Director for the Leadership for Health Improvement Programme being piloted by the Department of Health.

Alison McCallum is Director of Public Health and Health Policy at NHS Lothian in Edinburgh, Scotland. Her responsibilities include leading efforts to protect and improve health and reduce health inequalities across Lothian. She previously worked at the National Research and Development Centre for Welfare and Health, Helsinki, Finland, and Department of Public Health, University of Helsinki, where she combined research and teaching with giving advice to national and Nordic bodies.

John Øvretveit is Director of Research at the Medical Management Centre, the Karolinska Institute, Stockholm, and Professor of Health Policy and Management at Bergen University Medical School, Norway, and previously at the Nordic School of Public Health, Gothenburg, Sweden. His recent book describes action evaluation methods for giving rapid feedback to service providers and policy-makers to improve their services.

Paul Plsek is a private consultant in quality management and creative thinking working with many industries, including the health sector. An engineer by background, he was formerly an engineering manager at Bell Laboratories and the corporate quality planning director for AT&T. Since becoming a consultant he has worked for, among others, Kaiser Permanente, the UK National Health Service, and the national health system in Sweden.

John Wilkinson is Director of the North East Public Health Observatory, based in Durham University, one of nine public health observatories that were created in England in 2000. He was chair of the Association of Public Health Observatories from 2002 to 2006. A general practitioner for a number of years before entering public health, he has worked in public health in both service and academic environments.

Series preface

In almost all Western countries, health care is in a state of radical transformation. How can we meet the needs and demands of increasingly empowered 'consumers', contain costs, incorporate 'evidence based' modes of working, and re-motivate health care professionals – and all at the same time? The health care systems in Western countries are usually compared and contrasted along their axes of difference: nationalized versus fully market driven; tax-based versus insurance-based financing; 'gatekeeping' general practitioners versus self-referral to hospital care. Yet, with the exception perhaps of the USA, these health care systems are struggling in strikingly similar ways to achieve the optimal balance between market incentives and government controls; and between professional self-regulation and explicit accountability to patients and payers. It has become clear that simple solutions will not work: neither 'the market' nor 'state control' offers the complete answer to the challenges that face us. Equally, neither 'professional self-regulation' nor 'paying for performance' offers the simple recipe that will heal our health care systems' woes.

New models of health policy and health management are needed throughout the Western world, including a shift from a downstream preoccupation with health care services to an upstream focus on the health of communities and its improvement, tackling the widening 'health gap' between social groups; novel conceptions of organizing integrated care and chronic disease management; new approaches to performance management; innovative and realistic information management; effective human resource management; new models for managing clinical work; and so forth. These new models and approaches need to be theoretically sound, empirically based, and speak to professionals and patients and the problems facing them.

There is a great and urgent need for leadership in health and health care, and the many managers and professionals who end up in health management roles currently lack a well-defined series of textbooks to equip them with the requisite knowledge and insights derived from experience and research. We do not need more management hype, or yet another management fad or fashion that is unthinkingly applied to health care. These days more than ever, however, we do need to learn from each other's experiences and mistakes, and we need to be able to communicate and build upon 'best practices' developed elsewhere.

The *Routledge Health Management Series* aims to meet these needs by providing health care managers with the theoretical knowledge, practical insights and concrete examples they require in today's rapidly changing health care environment, including experiences from adjacent fields (e.g. business, service industry, and so forth) where relevant. The series has a strong international orientation, comparing related developments and drawing on examples from different countries. The series is aimed at Masters students, other postgraduate students and also at experienced managers providing them with an up-to-date overview of the latest developments in their particular field(s) of interest. The books in the series contain a balanced mix of theoretical backgrounds and starting points on the one hand, and practice-oriented advice and guidance on the other in order to show how these theoretical concepts might be applied to concrete management challenges. Finally, each book pays explicit attention to the 'practitioner perspective': each book contains direct accounts or case studies, often written by practitioners, of the relevance (or otherwise) to them of the issues presented.

Prof. Dr. Mac Berg, MD, PhD
Prof. Dr. Robbert Huijsman, MBA, PhD
Prof. Dr. David J. Hunter, MA, PhD, HonFPHM, FRCP(Edin.)
Prof. Dr. John Øvretveit, PhD

Acknowledgements

This book has benefited greatly from the contributions from my co-authors, all of whom write from their particular public health expertise. I want to thank them for their generous responses to my invitation to write, for meeting deadlines and for the quality of their contributions, which made my task as editor considerably easier. I am also immensely grateful as ever to Christine Jawad who has assisted with formatting the text and sorting out various loose ends in order to complete the manuscript. Finally, I'd like to thank the health management series editor at Routledge, Francesca Heslop, and her colleague, Emma Joyes, for their enthusiastic support for this book and for their forbearance throughout its compilation.

David J. Hunter
August 2006

Introduction

This book is about the struggle taking place in many health care systems around the world to rebalance their policies and practices away from an almost exclusive focus on downstream health care to one that gives increasing priority to an upstream focus on health. The word 'struggle' is used advisedly. In his annual report for 2005, the Chief Medical Officer for England, Sir Liam Donaldson, reports a dismal situation as far as the state of public health in England is concerned. He writes:

> In talking extensively to public health professionals throughout the NHS over the past two years, the following points consistently emerge from their accounts:
>
> ■ Expressed commitment to public health by many health bodies is not matched by concerted action.
> ■ Public health budgets are regularly 'raided' to find funding to reduce hospital financial deficits or to meet productivity targets in clinical services.
> ■ Valued small-scale local projects to improve health are often not sustained, losing funding and the skills that had been acquired over time.
>
> (Department of Health 2006: 40)

Though essential to protect and improve the health of the population as well as to reduce health inequalities, and as the CMO for England makes clear, public health services 'are vulnerable, in ways that clinical specialties are not, to lack of growth, to the effects of repeated management reorganisation and to the compelling and emotive competition for resources from clinical services' (Department of Health 2006: 43). It is a familiar story that is repeated in various studies of public health policy and practice (Wanless 2004; Hunter and Marks 2005). Yet the paradox is that public health continues to remain weak at a time when it should be strong. People throughout Europe and elsewhere are fatter, less physically and mentally fit, consume too much alcohol, and indulge in sexual behaviour that has given rise to a significant increase in sexually transmitted infections.

The argument in favour of investment in public health is, at its core, a simple one: why spend significant resources (financial and human) on fixing people when they fall ill when in the vast majority of cases it would be more cost-effective and enhance the quality of life of people if the causes of ill-health could be avoided in the first place. As the story goes, why do we spend our time and effort downstream rescuing people from the river once they have fallen in instead of going upstream to discover what is causing them to fall into the river in the first place?

But it is not enough to consider the policy context and the challenges it presents to policy-makers and others. Considerable and complex though these are, effective public health action cannot succeed on the scale required and on a sustainable basis without a workforce that is 'fit for purpose'. Hence the need to ensure that good management and leadership are in place to allow the effective implementation of policy to have at least a chance of succeeding. For the most part, public health practitioners lack the change management and health improvement skills to translate the knowledge they have acquired through training into practice (Hunter 2002). Part of the difficulty lies in the nature of what constitutes public health, whose job it is and which types of interventions are effective. There is a risk of public health being 'everybody's business' and 'nobody's responsibility'. How to guard against this without being overly reductionist in the process and oversimplifying a complex reality is just one of the many challenges confronting policy-makers and managers.

There is also a need to get the balance right between individual and collective responsibility, an issue that is to the fore in much contemporary public health policy. And even when the need for collective action is accepted, knowing which levers to pull and to what effect often remains uncertain. Despite the considerable public health challenges faced by the Victorians in the nineteenth century, they were also comparatively easy to correct and the collective solutions easy to identify once the political will had been secured – whether it was a matter of purifying water, constructing a sewage system, or clearing slum dwellings. Policy-makers in the twenty-first century feel less unequivocal about how to act, perceiving public health problems like obesity, smoking, alcohol abuse, diabetes and so on as questions of individual lifestyle where the role of government is limited to one of facilitating and enabling change in behaviour. Hence the search for new techniques and services, like social marketing and health trainers, to bring about a change in individual lifestyles. Such a search is fuelled by a perception that people do not welcome strong government meddling in their personal lives – nor do they trust government to act in their best interests. So new and more subtle means are needed to help people change their behaviour. But not all observers perceive the role of government to be so limited and unwelcome. They consider that legislative action, for example, can help to change a culture as it did in respect of road safety when the wearing of seat belts was made compulsory. They do not accept that collective decisions are merely the sum total of millions of individual decisions and consider that governments have a stewardship function in promoting and protecting the health of their populations.

Even if it is acknowledged that governments should and can act, there is another balance to be achieved between the public health contribution of health care services on the one hand and the contribution of non-health care services on the other. For the most part, the contribution of health care to health improvement has been overlooked. In its place has been a polarized debate between those who favour action by health services on the one hand and those who focus on the wider determinants of health on the other. This may be unhelpful. If the ability of health care to increase life expectancy and alleviate suffering is significant then this needs to be acknowledged and acted upon. Health care services can also mitigate inequalities in health although their history has been one of a widening health gap. Whatever the appeal of changing society and the environment, it does not follow that health services have little role to play (Bunker 2001).

The fact that the public health field is riven with so many uncertainties and imponderables, together with matters of balance and political judgement, is what contributes to the enormity and complexity of the health improvement challenge. A possibly unique, and certainly unusual, feature of the book is the combination of policy analysis and management development in respect of what it means to manage for health. Invariably textbooks deal with either the policy environment and context or the needs of, and skills required by, practitioners and others to function effectively – but rarely both in combination. Yet context is a critical determining factor in shaping policy and in ensuring its effective delivery. Without a sound understanding of context and the drivers of policy, the ability of those charged with managing for health to operate effectively is much diminished. Many of the difficulties in management are not simply technical in nature (e.g. poor competences and limited experience) but result from a dysfunctional or malfunctioning policy and organizational context. Effective management practice cannot sensibly be divorced from such a context. Hence the book's purpose to bring the two elements together in a single integrated text in order to demonstrate the interaction between policy context and management practice.

Although the book concentrates on developments in the United Kingdom, where there exists a strong and well-developed public health function, and where policy and practice developments have been most marked and well documented, occasional reference is made to developments elsewhere in Europe and North America that are wrestling with similar concerns and dilemmas. Moreover, two of the chapters have been written by academic researchers based at the Karolinska Institute in Stockholm, Sweden. Many of the policy innovations in public health have been pioneered in the Scandinavian countries. Finally, the underlying core themes and principles with which the book is concerned have a much wider resonance and applicability and are not country or health system-specific.

LEADERSHIP AND MANAGEMENT

At this point, a brief word on the distinction between the terms 'leadership' and 'management' is called for since they often give rise to confusion. The title of the book has opted for the term 'managing' rather than 'leading', although using the latter term would have been entirely appropriate and from time to time it appears in what follows. However, it was decided to stick with 'managing' to make the point that public health practitioners often lack the essential management skills to enable them to become successful and respected leaders. In many respects, public health has not been short of heroic leaders. During its 'golden age' in the Victorian era, public health produced many such individuals who took issue with the disparities in health evident between social groups and who mobilized the evidence to ensure action. Among these so-called 'Victorian visionaries' were Joseph Bazalgette (responsible for starting the sewer system in London), Joseph Chamberlain (who called for land reform, housing reform and higher taxes on the rich), Edwin Chadwick (who was responsible for bringing the Public Health Act of 1848 onto the statute book), John Snow (famous for the Broad Street pump episode), and William Henry Duncan (who became Liverpool's, and the country's, first Medical Officer of Health).

In contrast to the considerable achievements of these often remarkable Victorian leaders, the leadership challenge in contemporary public health is a very different and much more complex one. A reliance on heroic individuals is therefore neither appropriate nor possible, even if it were desirable. Leadership groups are required in a modern public health context. A further point to stress is that effective leadership for health demands a good grasp of change management skills, and these have not for the most part been well understood or developed in the public health workforce (Hunter 2003).

More generally, there is a well-trodden and continuing debate in the literature concerning the relationship between management and leadership, and in particular where one ends and the other begins. Goodwin usefully reviews the key components of the distinction between management and leadership (Goodwin 2006: 6–9). Although these need not detain us here, he makes the point that despite management and leadership often being very different, they are not mutually exclusive. Some academics go further and regard leadership as an integral part of the manager's role. The most eloquent exponent of this view is Henry Mintzberg who is critical of the windy rhetoric that surrounds a great deal of thinking on leadership. For example, he uses the terms interchangeably despite the fashion to distinguish them on the grounds that 'leadership is supposed to be something bigger, more important' (Mintzberg 2004: 6). Mintzberg rejects this distinction, as indeed this book does, 'simply because managers have to lead and leaders have to manage. Management without leadership is sterile; leadership without management is disconnected and encourages hubris' (2004: 6). So, in keeping with this refusal to cede management to leadership the title of the book has been chosen accordingly.

PLAN OF THE BOOK

Chapter 1 sets the policy context for the management challenge in public health and health improvement. Subsequent chapters, in their various ways, seek to illuminate the issues and tensions set out in this scene-setting chapter and to offer ways by which they might be managed better to the benefit of the public health function. A number of contributing authors have been enlisted to write selected chapters and they are named accordingly below.

Chapter 2 examines the contemporary public health function and infrastructure, and reviews criticisms of its overall 'fitness for purpose' and the deficits that need addressing. It argues that a better understanding of the nature and composition of the public health workforce is called for in order to identify gaps and deficits in its skill mix prior to strengthening capacity and capability. Given the diverse nature of the public health function and those engaged in its practice, the importance of sound and appropriate management is now being recognized.

Chapter 3 explores what managing for health entails at national and sub-national levels and the models of management that might assist in the task. It is critical of the new public management thinking that has dominated health policy and the reform of health systems over the past decade or so, and argues for a different approach to management and in particular to managing for health, drawing on complexity science theory and health improvement knowledge. The public health system is viewed as a complex adaptive system.

Chapter 4, through the presentation of a detailed case study, considers many of the complex challenges facing contemporary public health and those charged with managing the function. The authors, Mats Brommels and Alison McCallum, also consider some of the qualities and skills public health managers need to operate effectively in such a complex setting. They articulate a postmodernist perspective on management that moves away from a preoccupation with traditional conceptions of management to embrace notions of complexity.

Chapter 5 reviews issues in the sphere of information, intelligence and knowledge management in respect of public health since these are critical to a successful and effective public health function. John Wilkinson and Kathryn Bailey comment on the extensive sources of information that exist and provide details of sources and how to access these. A recurring theme of the chapter is that despite the existence of numerous datasets and knowledge banks they are under-utilized in practice. The chapter calls for more data-literate managers.

Chapter 6 examines the prospect of achieving a research-informed public health and shows through examples how research can help inform public health management decisions. John Øvretveit assesses the place of evidence in public health policy and decision-making. He believes that evidence-based public health is neither desirable nor feasible, which is why the emphasis should be on a more research-informed public health.

Chapter 7 reviews the implications for management training and development in respect of those practising public health. It briefly describes some of the management and leadership programmes on offer. However, most of the chapter is devoted to a case study of a new programme – the Leadership for Health Improvement Programme (LHIP) – that is being piloted in the North of England during 2006–7 with support from the Department of Health in England. The architects and organizers of the programme, Catherine Hannaway, Paul Plsek and David Hunter, describe the three knowledge domains that go to make up the LHIP. The programme's pedagogy and curriculum are derived from health improvement knowledge principles that have been applied in recent years to health care services in many countries, including the United States, United Kingdom and several European health systems. Through a series of intensive modules, the leadership programme seeks to illustrate the value of improvement tools and techniques in securing a more effective approach to leadership and management in public health.

Chapter 8 brings together the key themes and issues from the preceding chapters and looks ahead to the future and what it is likely to hold for public health managers and leaders as we move through the twenty-first century.

Finally, each chapter includes key points, discussion questions for readers who may wish to reflect on what they have read and apply the issues to their work setting, and a full list of references.

REFERENCES

Bunker, J.P. (2001) *Medicine matters after all*. London: Nuffield Trust.

Department of Health (2006) *On the state of the public health: annual report of the Chief Medical Officer 2005*. London: Department of Health.

Goodwin, N. (2006) *Leadership in health care: a European perspective*. London: Routledge.

Hunter, D.J. (2002) Management and public health, in R. Detels, J. McEwen, R. Beaglehole and H. Tanaka (eds) *Oxford textbook of public health: the methods of public health*, Volume 2, 4th edition. Oxford: Oxford University Press.

Hunter, D.J. (2003) *Public health policy*. Cambridge: Polity.

Hunter, D.J. and Marks, L. (2005) *Managing for health: what incentives exist for NHS managers to focus on wider health issues?* London: King's Fund.

Mintzberg, H. (2004) *Managers not MBAs: a hard look at the soft practice of managing and management development.* Harlow: Prentice-Hall.

Wanless, D. (2004) *Securing good health for the whole population*, Final Report. London: HM Treasury.

7

Chapter 1

The policy context and growing importance of health

David J. Hunter

[W]e are entering a new era in which the public health perspective will become more central to the health development agenda.

Beaglehole and Bonita (2004: 253)

KEY POINTS OF THIS CHAPTER

- Health systems globally are grappling with a range of shared policy and management challenges
- Epidemiological and demographic evidence shows that chronic disease and public health are the two major priorities facing health systems in the twenty-first century
- A major challenge confronting policy-makers is rebalancing health systems from a focus on health care and sickness to one on health and well-being
- To achieve this shift the public health function has to be 'fit for purpose', and there are doubts about whether the workforce possesses either the capacity or capability to deliver the necessary change

INTRODUCTION

Health systems throughout the world are grappling with a series of complex challenges, including growing demand for health care, rising public expectations, demographic trends that point to ageing populations, a constant flow of often expensive new treatments and interventions, and the introduction of cost containment measures in health care in an effort to manage the pressures on health systems.

In addition, epidemiological trends show populations across Europe and beyond becoming less healthy as 'diseases of comfort' (e.g. chronic diseases caused by an obesogenic environment) due to technological advance grow at an alarming rate, manifesting themselves as major public health problems in this century (Choi *et al.* 2005). A sharp rise in childhood obesity, resulting in an increase in health-related diseases such as diabetes, is matched by rapid increases in alcohol-related diseases and in sexually transmitted infections. In addition, infectious diseases have not disappeared and pandemics such as Avian bird flu threaten to occur at any time. As if these public health challenges were not enough, there are also the threats arising from a range of diverse concerns like toxic environments and bioterrorism.

As is quickly evident from this opening paragraph, the nature of public health is both 'expansive and rather amorphous' (Blank and Burau 2004: 174). It therefore poses considerable management and leadership challenges, perhaps even unique in terms of their scale and complexity, which are the subject of this book.

Until fairly recently, public health practitioners have tended to focus on the science and knowledge base of their craft and have rather neglected the application of that knowledge through management action. But this situation is changing and it is now accepted that those charged with improving the public's health need to be equipped with appropriate management skills. These are especially important in order to shift the balance from health care to health.

Despite the often complex differences in structure and funding, which seem to preoccupy students of comparative health policy and organization, countries across Europe and beyond are all confronting the same or similar policy conundrums and are urgently searching for solutions. Back in the 1940s when the British NHS was introduced it was naively assumed that once the backlog of illness and disease had been treated the population would be healthier and make fewer demands on finite health care resources. But the reformers underestimated the ability of the medical profession, the health technology industry and pharmaceutical companies to come up with new treatments to treat diseases that were hitherto untreatable or unknown. Health care became not just a matter of life and death but also of an improved quality of life – in World Health Organization (WHO) parlance, 'adding life to years' and not simply 'years to life'. Recent advances in, and the rapid growth of, cosmetic surgery are a vivid demonstration of how far health care has travelled over the past 30 years or so and the types of essentially lifestyle treatments that people demand. Such a preoccupation with health care, and its extension into areas that were only dimly foreseeable a few years ago, has tended to marginalize the importance of promoting and improving health, especially when investing in health requires long lead times and an acceptance that tangible, visible results may not be obvious.

Yet, despite the fact that most health policy tends to be focused on health care delivery, and on how primary and secondary services can be made more efficient and effective, there is a growing concern that there needs to be a rebalancing of policy away from downstream secondary care and towards upstream public health.

9

Many commentators and analysts believe that instead of repairing people once they become ill and treating symptoms, we should be focusing more of our efforts and scarce resources on preventing them from falling ill in the first place. This is especially so in the context of chronic or non-communicable disease, which is now regarded as the epidemic of our time (Horton 2005).

Confronting the powerful vested interests and public desire to consume acute health care possibly poses the greatest challenge to policy-makers and those charged with improving health. This book seeks to describe the nature of that challenge and to consider how it can be met more effectively through better management and leadership. Its central thesis is that managing and leading for health can be strengthened through the application of appropriate models of management and through equipping its practitioners with the requisite combination of hard and soft skills. However, the management task in public health is, even by health policy standards, an exceptional one as we shall see. Context is all-important, which is why it is essential to understand the environment in which public health and health improvement are organized and delivered.

THE RISE OF HEALTH IN HEALTH POLICY

From time to time in the evolution of health policy, concern over the state of the public's health results in public health rising up the policy agenda with governments anxious to demonstrate a commitment not just to making sick people well but to keeping people well and preventing them from falling ill. As a former US Surgeon-General, C. Everett Koop, once famously remarked, 'health care is vital to all of us some of the time but public health is vital to all of us all of the time'. In many countries, including the UK, we are witnessing one of those periods in the history of public health when it occupies centre stage (Baggott 2005; Hunter 2003). However, occupying such a position is not an unalloyed blessing and brings with it both opportunities and challenges. Nor is it free from numerous contradictions and paradoxes, as we shall see. Notable among these is that even when public health concerns break through to public attention, they tend not to have much staying power; or the solutions quickly get reduced to individual lifestyle changes rather than changes involving income redistribution and other social policy interventions (Mechanic 2003). As Frankford (2003: 511) succinctly puts it: 'population health arouses little passion, unless it starts redistributing income, in which case the passion is oppositional'.

To reinforce the point, we (that is, the body politic) have been here many times before. No sooner has public health achieved prominence than it is just as rapidly relegated to the sidelines, swept aside as the recurring problems of health care services reassert themselves and once again absorb the attention of policy-makers.

As has often been apparent throughout its history, the danger is always present that 'the management of financial resources and waiting lists will continue to dominate the day to day agenda of the NHS' (Dalziel 2000: 703). In such a context, Dalziel asks, 'how can the principles of health improvement become truly influential in this agenda, not only for the health service but also across government?' (2000: 703).

Not least among the challenges is ensuring that the new-found interest in, and commitment to, public health can be sustained for a sufficient period of time to enable the policy rhetoric to become practical reality. The danger in the fast-moving world of policy change and short-term electoral cycles is that the interest in public health, which demands a long-term commitment, will once again prove short-lived. Indeed, at the time of writing there are already signs of that occurring within the NHS in England.

The reasons for a growing interest in public health lie primarily in an acknowledgement of what has been termed 'the neglected epidemic' of chronic disease, as well as mounting concern over the increasing cost of health care services and the need to shift the paradigm towards health improvement and prevention in order to manage demands on health care more effectively. Without such a shift, publicly funded health systems are likely to prove unsustainable. Indeed, the British prime minister comes close to admitting as much in a major speech on healthy living in which he points to the fact that an estimated 1.7 million people in the UK have type 2 diabetes, with 10 per cent of NHS resources used to treat diabetes (Blair 2006). This could double by 2010. At the same time, it has been noted that a widening gap exists between the reality of chronic disease worldwide and the response of national governments to it (Strong *et al.* 2005). Yet, in 2005, all chronic diseases accounted for 72 per cent of the total global burden of disease in the population aged 30 years and older. Chronic disease rates are higher in the Russian Federation and low-income and middle-income countries than in Canada or the UK.

To understand the origins of a renewed focus on public health that is evident in many health systems, a good starting point is the 1970s. This decade witnessed something of an international revival of interest in public health policy and one that echoed what many of the Victorian visionaries already knew – namely, the importance of the wider determinants of health and the contribution to health improvement from pure water, effective sewage disposal, food hygiene, decent housing and a safe working environment. The decade was notable for the appearance of two major influential documents: the Lalonde report in Canada, and the World Health Organization's *Health For All* initiative. Since these landmark documents, and others that appeared some years later, notably WHO's Ottawa Charter in 1986, public health has never been far from the policy agenda, although only rarely has it occupied centre stage and been able to assert itself successfully against the overwhelming pressure exerted by health care systems centred on hospitals and beds (Hunter 2003). As a consequence of these developments in the 1970s, all countries have detailed policies for public health. Reducing inequalities in health is also an aim of most of these policies. However, whether these policies are for serious implementation or are merely an example of gesture politics is perhaps a more pertinent question to pose.

Despite being a fertile period in the evolution of public health, the 1970s was also a paradoxical and frustrating one. In terms of policy thinking at this time the renaissance of public health seemed confident and assured, but was in striking contrast to the changes occurring in its organization and structure that were having precisely the opposite effect. Public health was at serious risk of losing its way and its ability to implement successfully the policy opportunities that were beginning to open up. Indeed, this conundrum is something of a recurring one in the recent history of public health.

The Lalonde report

The publication of the report by the Canadian Minister of Health, Marc Lalonde, in 1974 heralded a new dawn for public health with its radical and enlightened thinking and critique of modern health care systems (Lalonde 1974). The report proved seminal as it was the first government document in the Western world to acknowledge that the emphasis on a biomedical model of health care was neither desirable for the enhancement of health nor relevant to prevention. What was radical about the agenda was its focus on an 'upstream' policy perspective. Future improvements in the health of Canadians would, it was claimed, come mainly from improvements in the environment, moderating risky lifestyles, and increasing our understanding of human biology. Its intellectual underpinnings were inspired by the work of Thomas McKeown whose thesis was that modern medicine was too disease focused and overly concerned with the individual at the expense of taking a holistic view, and ignored the wider socio-economic and environmental determinants of health (McKeown 1979).

The Lalonde report introduced the 'health field concept' as the basis for rebalancing health policy away from a preoccupation with health care and towards a concern with the environment and lifestyle. The 'health field concept' was not faultless and attracted its critics, who took issue with what was in their view the misplaced emphasis on individual lifestyle factors that could lead to 'victim-blaming'. Structural socio-economic factors as key determinants of health received insufficient attention. Not all the factors and pressures affecting health status were amenable to individual influence or decision. Over thirty years later, similar heated debates between the collective and individual continue to rage and shape policy, as we shall see.

Whatever its shortcomings, the Lalonde report became a touchstone for all those reformers committed to a 'whole systems' approach to health policy in which there was a search for a new equilibrium between health care considerations and those affecting the wider health of the population. Sadly, since the Lalonde report, and despite all the praise lavished upon it, progress in shifting the paradigm has been underwhelming and, as two commentators have concluded, there has been 'a logjam in health policy' (Legowski and McKay 2000). In the end, Lalonde failed to break the mould or shift the policy paradigm, and the prevailing bias in favour of health care services and the vested interests associated with them have continued more or less unabated.

Elsewhere, including the UK, the policy response to the 'new public health' thinking which emerged in the 1970s was far less ambitious. Like Lalonde, the equivalent report from the government, published in 1976, was a product of economic restraint and pressures on resources (Department of Health and Social Security 1976). Unlike Lalonde, its impact remained muted. It did not make specific recommendations for policy change but was intended merely 'to start people thinking and talking about the place of prevention in the overall, longer term development of the health and related services'. Nevertheless, it sought to stress that 'prevention is better than cure' and paved the way some sixteen years later for the first ever health strategy for England.

WHO initiatives

During this period other important initiatives kept the notion of public health and healthy public policy alive. First, there was the WHO *Health for All* concept that was introduced at the 1978 International Conference on Primary Health Care in Alma-Ata (in the former USSR) (WHO 1978). The Declaration of Alma-Ata is widely regarded as a seminal document, and is still referred to as a touchstone in the evolution of public health policy. The Declaration was built on some years later during a WHO conference on health promotion in 1986, which gave rise to the Ottawa Charter (WHO 1986). The Charter identified five action areas:

- to build healthy public policy by making healthy choices easy for the community;
- to create supportive environments, including the provision of affordable housing and effective transport policy;
- to strengthen community action by empowering communities to be involved in health promotion activities;
- to develop personal skills through education, information and life-skills training;
- to achieve the reorientation of health care services.

The overall aim of the Charter was to secure a better balance between curative and preventive services, accompanied by training professionals to appreciate the social and environment determinants of health.

Developments in the UK

The first health strategy in England appeared in 1992 (Secretary of State for Health 1992). It was preceded some years earlier by the first health strategy in the UK produced by the devolved administration responsible for health in Wales (Welsh Health Planning Forum 1989a, 1989b). The English strategy, *Health of the Nation* (HOTN), was remarkable not only for being the first strategy of its kind but for being produced by a Conservative government not renowned for its commitment either to central planning or to the broader health agenda. This was, after all, a government that did not subscribe to the notion of health inequalities or believe that poverty might have something to do with the widening health gap between social groups. Up until then, most of the government's energies had been devoted to introducing an internal market into the NHS. The attempt to talk publicly about the importance of health rather than health care echoed the discussions in the 1970s at the time of the Lalonde report. Upon its publication, health ministers and officials insisted that HOTN was 'shifting the focus from NHS institutions and service inputs to people and health' (Mawhinney and Nichol 1993: 45). HOTN also sought to widen the responsibility for health across government, although its origins were firmly rooted in the Department of Health and the NHS, both regarded as the natural leads for public health.

There was an international significance to HOTN as well. It acknowledged its debt to the World Health Organization's (WHO) *Health for All* approach in its overarching goal to add years to life and life to years. In turn, WHO cited HOTN as a model strategy that demonstrated how governments could act to improve population health.

HOTN was generally welcomed, although not devoid of criticism that centred on two issues: first, a failure to take into account socio-economic determinants of health, and, second, the pursuit of a largely disease-based model of health in respect of the strategy's thrust and the targets set. Two commentators wanted the targets and activities to focus on the factors that led to ill-health – smoking, poverty, inadequate housing, for example – rather than on the diseases and conditions that resulted (Holland and Stewart 1998).

HOTN heralded a commitment to target-setting that was to remain a feature of all subsequent health strategies, and, indeed, of public policy more generally under subsequent governments. Such an overly prescriptive approach to managing performance, whereby targets were determined by the centre and imposed on health authorities, was criticized for being inflexible and inhibiting implementation (Barnes and Rathwell 1993; Hunter 2002). Such an approach was also felt to concentrate on the measurable to the exclusion of the unmeasurable.

Despite its significance as, in the words of the National Audit Office, an 'ambitious and far-reaching' strategy, the implementation of HOTN proved less successful (Department of Health 1998). When the performance of the NHS was being judged,

HOTN did not seem to figure. What mattered far more were the by now familiar preoccupations with reducing waiting lists, ensuring speedy access to hospital beds, and keeping within budget. Whenever the going got tough, public health would be among the first casualties as managers focused on the 'must do's' affecting acute care services. Whether or not it is regarded as an appropriate style of management, they were not brought to heel for failing to meet HOTN targets.

New government, new strategies

New Labour entered office in May 1997 promising a paradigm shift in health policy. Not only would there be no more 'big bang' structural reforms of the NHS but at the top of its priorities would be public health. To emphasize the point, a new post of public health minister was created in England within the Department of Health but not elsewhere in the UK. Political devolution to Wales, Scotland and Northern Ireland in 2000 meant that health policy became a devolved responsibility, with political leadership being exercised from Cardiff, Edinburgh and Belfast.

The new government was keen to show its commitment to a more socially equitable and cohesive society that involved the efforts of all government departments and not only health. It became publicly acceptable to talk about health inequalities and the social determinants of health. Indeed, the Chancellor of the Exchequer assumed a prominent role in the assault on poverty and inequality, especially among children, with a commitment to end child poverty by 2020. A range of policies, including Sure Start, the welfare-to-work programme, tax credits, national minimum wage, and national strategy for neighbourhood renewal, were all intended to tackle social deprivation and poor health.

As part of its determination to do things differently, the public health minister commissioned an independent review of the evidence base in tackling health inequalities from a former chief medical officer for England, Sir Donald Acheson, in order to advise where government should focus its attention (Independent Inquiry into Inequalities in Health 1998). Of the review's 39 recommendations, only three directly concerned the NHS or were within its power to influence directly (Macintyre 2000).

Part of the government's response lay in producing a successor strategy to HOTN (Secretary of State for Health 1999). Although the strategy, which eventually appeared in its final form in 1999, was concerned with settings in health, like the workplace, school and community, some commentators were disappointed that it belonged firmly to a health care model that was less about supporting communities to remain healthy than about keeping individuals alive (Fulop and Hunter 1999). Repeating a perceived flaw in HOTN, the new strategy was focused mainly on disease-based areas such as cancer, coronary heart disease/stroke and mental illness, with targets similarly disease based. Just as HOTN found that the dominance of the medical model underlying it proved to be a major barrier to its ownership by agencies outside the health sector, notably local government and voluntary agencies, so a similar fate seemed destined to befall its successor.

The appearance of a new strategy to replace HOTN did not complete the government's public health policy-making. Far from it. As the government moved into a new decade and century, the flow of policies increased with an urgency and energy that rather bewildered managers and practitioners among others. A key contribution to thinking about public health was the work of Derek Wanless, former chair of the National Westminster Bank, who was invited by the Chancellor of the Exchequer to advise on future health trends over a 20-year period and on the ability of a health service funded by central taxation to meet whatever challenges lay ahead.

In the first of two reports, Wanless gave an unexpected prominence to the importance of public health. His argument was that good health and good economics – health and wealth – went together. More specifically, his report maintained that 'better public health measures could significantly affect the demand for health care' (Wanless 2002: 1.27). On top of any health benefits, a focus on public health was seen to bring wider benefits by increasing productivity and reducing inactivity in the working-age population. In terms of the overall balance of care, Wanless was critical of the prevailing bias in favour of acute hospital care.

Such a bias in health policy is by no means unique to the UK. In its *World Health Report 2002*, the World Health Organization points out that much scientific effort and most health resources are directed towards treating disease rather than preventing it (WHO 2002). It calls on governments, in their stewardship role, to achieve a much better balance between preventing disease and merely treating its consequences. Lack of political will, not knowledge, is hindering progress.

The Wanless analysis and his recommendation that the government act to reduce demand on health care by promoting health were accepted by the government. However, the programme mapped out was an ambitious one and required a step change in the delivery of health policy.

Indeed, so keen was the government to demonstrate its commitment to a new approach and to a rebalancing of health policy in the direction charted by Wanless that he was invited to review progress the following year. It was of course far too soon to make robust judgements about the success of his strategy, but in his second report Wanless (2004) focused on the public health system in its widest sense and produced a powerful critique of the public health function.

The government's response to Wanless's second report was to deflect attention from it by immediately announcing that a new health strategy would be produced to which the public would be invited to contribute through a major consultation exercise. Many public health practitioners and policy commentators queried whether a new strategy was required, since the existing one – *Saving lives: our healthier nation* – had yet to be implemented and had already suffered from being sidelined by the priority targets in health care services, none of which affected public health (Hunter and Marks 2005).

In late 2004, on the back of the Wanless report which appeared in February of that year, the government published its revised health strategy for England, *Choosing health: making healthy choices easier* (Secretary of State for Health 2004). It marked a significant, though not widely reported, departure in terms of how the government saw its role in health improvement. Whereas its earlier strategy had emphasized the dual approach between government and individuals in promoting health, the new strategy shifted the focus much more firmly and explicitly towards the individual. The language around choice and for individual responsibility in leading healthier lives was new, and, rather than government exercising a leadership role, as envisaged in *Our Healthier Nation* and in WHO's Health Development Report, the role of government had been recast as a more modest enabling, facilitating one designed to provide advice and information in order to support individuals in making healthier choices. It marked a significant shift in public health thinking, albeit one in keeping with the government's overall approach to public policy and public sector reform. What has been termed the 'marketisation of policy' was being applied to health as to other areas of government policy (Bobbitt 2003; Hunter 2005). From about 2002, the government's reform rhetoric centred on devolution, putting power back to the front line, reducing central control, and giving patients and public more choice. The 1999 health strategy clearly needed updating to reflect the new language of political discourse and to bring thinking into line with the new mantra of choice and market-style incentives to modify lifestyles. Such thinking also dominates the most recent health policy strategy, which is concerned with shifting the balance from hospital to primary and community care (Secretary of State for Health 2006). As the strategy acknowledges, the issues raised are pertinent to public health since they are aimed at keeping people healthy and out of institutional care.

The example of the ban on smoking in public places illustrates the difference in approach well and the cautious nature of public health policy. In keeping with its emphasis on individual choice and desire not to be accused of being the 'nanny state', the English government was reluctant to take a lead on banning smoking. It was only when pressure began to mount, aided by a decision to ban smoking in Northern Ireland, Scotland and Wales, that ministers felt compelled to follow suit in England. However, even then the government left it to an open vote in Parliament to decide. But no less a person than the prime minister now accepts that government has a significant role in promoting population health:

> In formulating policy, I have undergone my own personal journey of change in this respect. A few years back, I would have hesitated long and hard over issues like the smoking ban. Now, and particularly where children are concerned, I have come to the conclusion we need to be tougher, more active in setting standards and enforcing them.
>
> (Blair 2006)

Developments in Wales and Scotland

The arrival of political devolution in 2000 gave a new impetus to UK health policy. Northern Ireland remains something of a special case at present pending a resolution of the political difficulties there. Until such time the devolved assembly has been suspended.

To a greater degree than is evident in England, Wales and Scotland have sought in their respective strategies to put health before health care (see, for example, National Assembly for Wales 2001; Scottish Executive 2003a, 2003b). What remains unclear is whether the strong rhetoric is, or will be, matched by developments on the ground. Greer, who has studied the development of public health in the devolved polities, is sceptical: Scotland is 'speaking of public health but still focusing on health care services', and Wales is 'focusing on integrated public health activities and promotion' (Greer 2001; 2006). It is also the case that Wales suffers from severe financial problems in its health care services that may prove too distracting to ignore in favour of putting health first.

It remains early days as far as devolution is concerned and as to whether it will result in a marked divergence in health policy as distinct from what happened under the former system of administrative devolution when policies and reforms varied at the margin but rarely in substance or in principle (Hunter and Wistow 1987; Hazell and Jervis 1998). Certainly, in respect of the smoking ban Scotland has shown the way within the UK and it seems likely that this may encourage the Scottish Executive to show similar bold leadership in respect of, for example, obesity. There is certainly talk of linking public health challenges to agendas around social justice and environmental sustainability. Despite much discussion of the need to merge these agendas, progress has been slow in England. It would be far easier to make the connections in the smaller UK countries. Moreover, while issues of globalization are as evident in Scotland and Wales as they are in England, the language of 'choice', 'markets' and 'competition' is absent from public discourse. There appears still to be a belief in, and support for, a public realm and a role for government in promoting the public good that remains distinctive. In these ways, at least, significant differences are evident across the UK, which is perhaps no longer as united as it once was.

Developments outside the UK

As noted at the start, more countries are concerned with issues surrounding health as distinct from health care and have produced health strategies and policies of varying quality and with varying degrees of commitment to their implementation. As a review of the health policies from 14 countries found, the policies are often detailed and ambitious but lack earmarked funding for implementing interventions (Crombie *et al.* 2003). The policies are usually accompanied by health targets that signal the direction in which improvements should occur and provide a mechanism for monitoring progress. Similar conclusions were reached by another study reviewing progress in eight countries in making decisions on public health (Allin *et al.* 2004). It reached three conclusions in particular. First, the political context within which public health policies are developed varies greatly. While the broad goals may be similar, including the strategies pursued, the political values guiding the choice of priorities vary greatly. Second, the countries differ with regard to the nature of the contemporary challenges to population health. The varying diets across countries provide one example. Third, and this is by no means confined to public health policy, the accounts of policy often assume a rational linear model of policy development and implementation that, upon closer scrutiny, is rarely the case.

What both these international studies clearly demonstrate are important weaknesses in the public health infrastructure. This includes information and surveillance systems, in addition to workforce issues, with regard to appropriate skill mix and related issues of capacity and capability. But public health is not only 'a field of knowledge but also a space for professional practice' (Frenk 1992: 73). Just as an effective information and intelligence system is essential in order to identify the emergence of health hazards and to determine whether policies are 'fit for purpose', there is also a critical need to ensure that appropriate mechanisms are in place to train practitioners to be able to implement policies and manage change. A long-standing criticism of public health is a failure to address such issues successfully. The reasons for this state of affairs and what might be done to remedy the situation are central themes of this book. Hence, the focus is less on the epidemiological dimensions of public health, or on the many worthy policies that can be found in various countries, and more on the mechanisms in place (or not in place) to secure effective management action. Health improvement strategies require a new approach to public health management and leadership. Later chapters will explore these issues at greater length. The remainder of this introductory chapter is devoted to the policy context and with the mismatch between policy intent and actual practice and outcomes. The review of these issues is intended to set the scene for the subsequent discussion of the requisite public health infrastructure needed and the training and development initiatives required to ensure it is embedded and sustained.

In his analysis of the new public health and the crisis afflicting it, Frenk (1992: 83) argues that our capacity to face the challenges of public health will require actions at the organization level and particular attention being paid to three issues: design, development and delivery. He argues for nothing short of the modernization of the public health function since its future 'will depend to a great extent on our ability to design and develop institutions and to ensure their sound performance'.

This is a theme echoed in the US Institute of Medicine's (IOM) wide-ranging critique of the public's health in the twenty-first century. The report concluded that 'the US is not fully meeting its potential in the area of population health' (Institute of Medicine 2003: 169). It argued that the public's health can only be supported through collective action, not through individual endeavour. The collective goods that are essential conditions for health can be secured only through organized action on behalf of the population (Gostin 2000). Another of its conclusions is that the protection and promotion of the population's health requires the public health infrastructure to be 'revitalised and strengthened' in respect of its 'human resources, information systems, and organisational capacity'. Achieving this goal requires preparing public health leaders with the appropriate skills and competencies. These will need to emphasize the cross-sectoral nature of the public health function since the actions and decisions of many agencies and levels of government affect population health. In addition to professional expertise in the specific subject area, and expertise in the core values and content of public health, competencies in leadership skills are essential. Yet it is often precisely these skills that remain ignored or undeveloped in preparing public health practitioners for the world they enter and the work they do. As the IOM report puts it, they must 'have mastery of the skills to mobilise, coordinate, and direct broad collaborative actions within the complex public health system' (Institute of Medicine 2003: 120). These skills are for 'vision, communication, and implementation'.

The IOM report asserted that health is a primary public good, because many aspects of human potential such as employment, social relationships, and political participation are contingent on it. Creating the conditions for people to be healthy should therefore be a shared social goal, and government has a special role in this, together with the contributions of other sectors of society.

A review of policies across Europe to tackle health inequalities found that despite some progress, many challenges remained (Judge *et al.* 2005). In particular, policies needed to be supported by financial and political commitment, as well as steps being taken to ensure that adequate capacity and infrastructure were in place to allow effective implementation to occur. Regardless of the precise nature of a policy or strategy, and the support that exists for it, if the means to implement it are either non-existent or inadequate in terms of capacity or capability, or both, then it will count for little. Wanless was struck by the mismatch between policy statements accumulating over some thirty years and a persistent failure to secure their rigorous implementation. The next chapter considers the public health function and its fitness for purpose in the twenty-first century. But not all the failure to promote health policy can be laid at the door of the public health function and its shortcomings. The nature and dynamics of health policy itself are problematic.

THE PARADOX OF HEALTH POLICY

As noted, even when favourably disposed towards public health the policy context has failed to provide a secure and sustained environment in which public health measures can be seriously implemented and tested. The paradox is that such a situation persists in the face of mounting evidence that the most significant improvements in health for populations (as distinct from individuals) have resulted from public health measures, not curative medicine (Fries *et al.* 1993). It is estimated that while 99 per cent of health spending in the US goes on medical care, this enormous expenditure prevents only 10 per cent of early deaths. In contrast, population-wide public health approaches have the potential to prevent around 70 per cent of early deaths through measures targeted at social, environmental and behavioural factors (Sulz and Young 1999). None of this is to decry the importance of medical care or its contribution to public health; rather, it is to argue in favour of achieving a proper balance between patient-centred and population-centred health care.

It is an argument that public health practitioners and campaigners, among others, have sought to advance, albeit without much success. In the UK a recent and powerful and unexpected champion for public health has been Derek Wanless, a former banker and hard-nosed businessman. In two important reports commissioned by the British government in 2002 and 2004 respectively, he sought to make the case for managing demand on acute care services by giving a higher priority to, and investing in, public health measures. Indeed, his central thesis was that the NHS, together with all health care services in the developed world, regardless of their funding mechanism, would become unaffordable within 20 years if there was a failure to stem the growing demand on it and manage it differently by giving priority to prevention and health improvement. His call is supported by the chief medical officer for England who has argued that despite the gains in longevity these may well prove short-lived as the next generation, as a result of unhealthy lifestyles, is destined to have a higher mortality rate, with children dying before their parents.

If there is general agreement that avoiding ill-health in the first place is a more successful way of promoting good health and prolonging quality of life, then it seems curious that the attention of policy-makers and managers and the resources they deploy are directed towards curative services. It puzzled Derek Wanless, too, when he concluded that despite 'numerous policy initiatives being directed towards public health they have not succeeded in rebalancing health policy away from the short-term imperatives of health care' (Wanless 2004: 6). Rather than a National Health Service, he claimed we have a 'National Sickness Service'. What accounts for such a state of affairs?

The reasons are multiple, although a dominant one has to be the power of the medical model in determining health policy priorities and resource flows. The hegemony of the medical profession has been extensively analysed and its power should not be underestimated, particularly when it operates in collusion with managers, the public and media (see, for example, Hunter 2006). Even the solutions to public health challenges such as obesity are seen to lie in biomedical or pharmaceutical responses. Or, in the case of high cholesterol levels (the result of unhealthy diets and lifestyles), the immediate answer, or 'quick fix', is seen to lie in prescribing statins to everyone over the age of 50. The medicalization of what are essentially social or lifestyle illnesses suggests that the medical model remains both powerful and attractive. In contrast, changing lifestyles requires behavioural change over a sustained period of time, which carries less appeal. Whereas drug therapies are likely to show quick results, environmental or lifestyle changes are likely to take far longer to demonstrate their impact and effectiveness.

But in seeking to understand the appeal of the medical model and curative health care, the presence and play of politics and power cannot be ignored. Often, in accounts of the medical model and even in discourses on management and leadership, the presence of power is overlooked, ignored or regarded as somehow distasteful and not appropriate for open discussion. Yet unless we overcome our ambivalence about power, and understand how it is exercised in particular circumstances and contexts, then we shall fail to understand fully why public health always seems to lurk in the shadows of medicine. After all, it was a Prussian pathologist turned anthropologist, Rudolf Virchow (quoted in Miller 1974: v), who famously wrote over a hundred years ago: 'medicine is a social science and politics nothing but medicine on a grand scale'. Organizations, including health systems, are funda-mentally political entities (Pfeffer 1992). Ignoring the realities of power and influence will not make them go away. Therefore, learning how to manage with power is so important – especially in rebalancing the health policy agenda in favour of health.

The play of power is evident in three of the six 'simple truths' Lewis *et al.* (2000) have identified in the operation of health care systems:

- *health care systems want to grow*: they are naturally expansionist and are inhabited by vested interests intent on survival and growth;
- *health care almost always wins out in the competition for resources*: this remains the case even when governments proclaim their commitment to improving health – it is not backed by a significant shift of resources even when such resources are 'promised';
- *changing the distribution of health status through 'upstream' strategies is extraordinarily difficult*: interventions intended to benefit the disadvantaged disproportionately benefit the already advantaged, thereby widening disparities and the health gap. More than 'upstream' single-sector interventions are required – rather, the policy focus needs to be on multisectoral strategies that address the broader determinants of health.

It is not difficult to understand why these simple truths ring true when it comes to public health policy and a failure of implementation. For a start, regarding the lead for public health as residing with the health care system immediately identifies public health with the medical model. Indeed, in some countries, notably the UK, for a long period of time public health was synonymous with public health medicine (see further Chapter 2). Only notions like the 'new public health' or 'wider public health', which appeared in the late 1970s and 1980s, sought to weaken the medical dominance and led to the notion of a multidisciplinary workforce in the pursuit of public health.

The simple truths also hold appeal because health improvement promises future, and often intangible, gains rather than immediate and visible ones, which in a political context governed by short-term considerations and electoral cycles poses a major impediment. It also challenges the status quo and the vested interests that profit from it. Whereas a switch from health care to improving health may strengthen social capital, the reverse may be true in the case of political capital. Moreover, the public, unless they were reprogrammed or their expectations transformed, would probably not look kindly upon politicians who failed to meet their perceived need for health care services.

To re-emphasize, this is not an attack on modern medicine *per se*, which is by no means ineffective and arguably has yet to realize its full potential in respect of its contribution to public health (Craig *et al.* 2006). It is, however, to insist that health care in the majority of developed countries has overestimated its effectiveness and underestimated its limitations (Palmer and Short 2000). Reforming health care systems, as governments are wont to do *ad nauseam*, will only result in limited gains in health in contrast to public health interventions that will transform the health status of whole communities. Nevertheless, the tension in policy between adopting an 'upstream' policy focus on the one hand that seeks to tackle the social and economic determinants of health, or a 'downstream' focus that seeks to make health services more concerned with health prevention and promotion remains evident. Achieving an optimal balance between these competing policy thrusts remains a key challenge for policy-makers since the uneasy coexistence of public health with health care services remains a major concern and arguably constitutes a significant barrier in successful policy implementation (Lewis 1986; Berridge 1999).

CONCLUSION

This review of the highlights of public health policy has established that many countries in Europe and elsewhere are actively engaged in giving a higher priority to public health and 'upstream' policy initiatives designed to improve the health of their populations. It has also shown, however, that for the most part countries are struggling to make their policies work in practice. In part this is an issue around the evidence base, but it is also a political issue in respect of the pressures on policy-makers stemming from 'downstream' health care services in which powerful and well-organized vested interests are able to exert considerable influence on the health system. Unless such influences are understood then building an effective public health function will fall short of what is required to shift the policy paradigm from health care to health.

DISCUSSION QUESTIONS

1   Do you think there is an unhelpful polarization between those who believe that health
    care has little role to play in improving health, on the one hand, and those who believe
    that intervening outside the health care sector is ineffective on the other? Is there a
    need for rebalancing these different strategies?
2   Do you think there remains a role for healthy public policy led by government, or is
    the government's emphasis on facilitating and enabling change among individuals
    correct?
3   If public health is always at risk of being sidelined or marginalized in health care
    systems because of the pressures from the acute care sector, should the lead role for
    public health be transferred to another sector or central department?

REFERENCES

Allin, S., Mossialos, E., McKee, M. and Holland, W. (2004) *Making decisions on public
health: a review of eight countries*. Brussels: European Observatory on Health
Systems and Policies.

Baggott, R. (2005) From sickness to health? Public health in England. *Public Money &
Management*, 25(4): 229–236.

Barnes, R. and Rathwell, T. (1993) *Study to assess progress in the adoption and
implementation of health goals and targets at the regional and local levels*. Leeds:
Nuffield Institute for Health, University of Leeds.

Beaglehole, R. and Bonita, R. (2004) Strengthening public health for the new era, in R.
Beaglehole (ed.) *Global public health: a new era*. Oxford: Oxford University Press,
pp. 253–268.

Berridge, V. (1999) *Health and society in Britain since 1939*. Cambridge: Cambridge
University Press.

Blair, T. (2006) Speech on healthy living, 26 July. www.number10.gov.uk/output/
Page9921.asp

Blank, R. and Burau, V. (2004) *Comparative health policy*. Basingstoke: Palgrave
Macmillan.

Bobbitt, P. (2003) *The shield of Achilles: war, peace and the course of history*. London:
Penguin.

Choi, B.C.K., Hunter, D.J., Tsou, W. and Sainsbury, P. (2005) Diseases of comfort: primary
cause of death in the 22nd century, *Journal of Epidemiology & Community Health*,
59(12): 1030–1034.

Craig, N., Weight, B., Hanlon, P. and Galbraith, S. (2006) Does health care improve health? *Journal of Health Services Research and Policy*, 11(1): 1–2.

Crombie, I.K., Irvine, L., Elliott, L. and Wallace, H. (2003) *Understanding public health policy: Learning from International Comparisons*. A Report to NHS Health Scotland. Dundee: University of Dundee.

Dalziel, M. (2000) Leadership for health. How can we ensure that the values and principles of public health become central to health and social policy? *Journal of Epidemiology & Community Health*, 43(9): 703–704.

Department of Health (1998) *The health of the nation – a policy assessed*. London: HMSO.

Department of Health and Social Security (1976) *Prevention and health: everybody's business: a reassessment of public and personal health*. A consultative document prepared jointly by the health departments of Great Britain and Northern Ireland. London: HMSO.

Frankford, D.M. (2003) Unchanging new leadership, *Journal of Health Policy, Politics and Law*, 28(2–3): 509–515.

Frenk, J. (1992) The new public health, in Pan American Health Organization, *The crisis of public health: reflections for debate*. Washington: PAHO/WHO, pp. 68–85.

Fries, J.F., Koop, C.E., Beadle, C.E., Cooper, P.P., England, M.J., Greaves, R.F., Sokolov, J.J. and Wright, D. (1993) Reducing health care costs by reducing the need and demand for medical services. *The New England Journal of Medicine*, 329(5): 321–325.

Fulop, N. and Hunter, D.J. (1999) Saving lives or sustaining the public's health? *British Medical Journal*, 319: 139–140.

Gostin, L.O. (2000) *Public health law: power, duty, restraint*. Berkeley and New York: University of California Press and Milbank Memorial Fund.

Greer, S. (2001) *Divergence and devolution*. London: Nuffield Trust.

Greer, S. (2006) The politics of health policy divergence, in J. Adams and K. Schmueker (eds) *Devolution in practice 2006: public policy differences within the UK*. Newcastle: IPPR North.

Hazell, R. and Jervis, P. (1998) *Devolution and health*. London: Nuffield Trust.

Holland, W.W. and Stewart, S. (1998) *Public health: the vision and the challenge*. London: Nuffield Trust.

Horton, R. (2005) The neglected epidemic of chronic disease. *The Lancet*, 5 October.

Hunter, D.J. (2002) England, in M. Marinker (ed.) *Health targets in Europe: polity, progress and promise*, London: BMJ Books, pp. 148–164.

Hunter, D.J. (2003) *Public health policy*. Cambridge: Polity.

Hunter, D.J. (2005) Choosing or losing health? *Journal of Epidemiology & Community Health*, 59: 1010–1013.

25

Hunter, D.J. (2006) From tribalism to corporatism: the continuing managerial challenge to medical dominance, in D. Kelleher, J. Gabe and G. Williams (eds) *Challenging medicine*, 2nd edition. London: Routledge, pp. 1–23.

Hunter, D.J. and Marks, L. (2005) *Managing for health: what incentives exist for NHS managers to focus on wider health issues?* London: King's Fund.

Hunter, D.J. and Wistow, G. (1987) *Community care in Britain: variations on a theme.* London: King Edward's Hospital Fund for London.

Independent Inquiry into Inequalities in Health (1998) *Report* (Acheson Report). London: HMSO.

Institute of Medicine (2003) *The future of the public's health in the 21st century.* Washington: National Academies Press.

Judge, K., Platt, S., Costongs, C. and Jurczak, K. (2005) *Health inequalities: a challenge for Europe.* London: UK Presidency of the EU.

Lalonde, M. (1974) *A new perspective on the health of Canadians.* Ottawa: Ministry of Supply and Services.

Legowski, B. and McKay, L. (2000) *Health beyond health care: twenty-five years of federal health policy development.* CPRN Discussion Paper No. H/04. Ottawa: Canadian Policy Research Networks.

Lewis, J. (1986) *What price community medicine? The philosophy, practice and politics of public health since 1919.* Brighton: Wheatsheaf.

Lewis, S., Saulnier, M. and Renaud, M. (2000) Reconfiguring health policy: simple truths, complex solutions, in G.L. Albrecht, R. Fitzpatrick and S.C. Scrimshaw (eds) *The Handbook of Social Studies in Health and Medicine.* London: Sage, pp. 509–523.

Macintyre, S. (2000) Modernising the NHS: prevention and the reduction of health inequalities. *British Medical Journal*, 320: 1399–1400.

McKeown, T. (1979) *The role of medicine: dream, mirage or nemesis,* 2nd edition. Oxford: Blackwell.

Mawhinney, B. and Nichol, D. (1993) *Purchasing for health: a framework for action.* London: NHS Management Executive.

Mechanic, D. (2003) Who shall lead: is there a future for population health? *Journal of Health Politics, Policy and Law*, 28(2–3): 421–442.

Miller, H. (1974) *Medicine and society.* Oxford: Oxford University Press.

National Assembly for Wales (2001) *Improving health in Wales: a plan for the NHS with its partners.* Cardiff: National Assembly for Wales.

Palmer, G.R. and Short, S.D. (2000) *Health care and public policy: an Australian analysis,* 3rd edition. Melbourne: Macmillan.

Pfeffer, J. (1992) *Managing with power: politics and influence in organisations.* Boston: Harvard Business School Press.

Scottish Executive (2003a) *Improving health in Scotland – the challenge.* Edinburgh: Scottish Executive.

Scottish Executive (2003b) *Partnership for care. Scotland's health white paper.* Edinburgh: Scottish Executive.

Secretary of State for Health (1992) *The health of the nation: A strategy for health in England.* Cm 1986. London: HMSO.

Secretary of State for Health (1999) *Saving lives: our healthier nation.* Cm 4386. London: HMSO.

Secretary of State for Health (2004) *Choosing health: making healthier choices easier.* Cm 6374. London: HMSO.

Secretary of State for Health (2006) *Our health, our care, our say: a new direction for community services.* Cm 6737. London: HMSO.

Strong, K., Mathers, C., Leeder, S. and Beaglehole, R. (2005) Preventing chronic diseases: how many lives can we save? *The Lancet,* 5 October.

Sulz, H.A. and Young, K.M. (1999) *Health care USA: understanding its organisation and delivery,* 2nd edition. New York: Aspen.

Wanless, D. (2002) *Securing our future health: taking a long-term view.* Final report. London: HM Treasury.

Wanless, D. (2004) *Securing good health for the whole population.* Final report. London: HM Treasury.

Welsh Health Planning Forum (1989a) *Strategic intent and direction for the NHS in Wales.* Cardiff: Welsh Office.

Welsh Health Planning Forum (1989b) *Local strategies for health: a new approach to strategic planning.* Cardiff: Welsh Office.

World Health Organization (WHO) (1978) *Declaration of Alma Ata.* Report of the International Conference on Primary Health Care. Geneva: WHO/Unicef.

World Health Organization (WHO) (1986) *First international conference on health promotion. The move towards a new public health: Ottawa charter for health promotion.* Ottawa: WHO/Health and Welfare Canada/Canadian Association for Public Health.

World Health Organization (WHO) (2002) *The World Health Report 2002: reducing risks, promoting healthy life.* Geneva: WHO.

Chapter 2

The public health function

David J. Hunter

KEY POINTS OF THIS CHAPTER

- Public health is difficult to define because of its scope and range
- Public health embraces three domains: health protection, health promotion and health service improvement
- To execute the various functions, public health has become a multidisciplinary workforce that is no longer based exclusively on a medical model or medically qualified practitioners who form only a small section of the workforce
- The multidisciplinary workforce may be said to function within a public health system at various levels – national, regional, local
- Strengthening the capacity and capability of public health is regarded as essential in the face of widespread concerns that the workforce lacks the requisite skills and competencies

INTRODUCTION

Perhaps both a strength and a weakness is the sheer scope of public health's remit. At one level, there is little that does not come within its purview. Getting some sense of the range and nature of the tasks and responsibilities confronting public health practitioners is therefore desirable before considering the management challenge facing the function and putting in place the necessary support. This chapter is in three sections. The first examines what is understood by public health and reviews the definitions that have been put forward over the years. These generally conceive of public health as broad and wide-ranging. The second section looks at what a public health system entails, since employing such a term may usefully demonstrate the particular challenges facing public health at different levels – national, regional and local. The final section considers issues surrounding the capacity and capability of public health and how they might be strengthened.

A particular dilemma facing public health concerns the perceived 'crisis' in public health arising from attempts by governments, and from the actions of other powerful groups, to redefine what constitutes the public realm. Such a redefinition can take many forms but may include relocating functions previously found in the public sector into the private sector, and also involve governments either seeking to withdraw altogether from functions previously undertaken by them or to reduce their stewardship or governance responsibilities adopting an enabling rather than a leadership function. All of these societal changes have major implications for the public health function and what is expected from it.

DEFINING PUBLIC HEALTH

Public health has been defined as 'the science and art of preventing disease, prolonging life, and promoting health through the organised efforts of society' (Acheson 1988). The definition is widely used and favoured because it is seen to reflect

> the essential elements of modern public health – a population perspective, an emphasis on collective responsibility for health and on prevention, the key role of the state linked to a concern for the underlying socio-determinants of health as well as disease, a multi-disciplinary basis . . . and an emphasis on partnership with the populations served.
>
> (Beaglehole and Bonita 1997: 221)

In his review of the public health function for the British government, Derek Wanless widened Acheson's definition by modifying the last part as follows: 'through the organised efforts and informed choices of society, organisations, public and private, communities and individuals' (Wanless 2004: 3). The revisions were intended to signal the social changes that had become manifest in an age of greater consumer choice, rising public expectations and a growing role for the private sector in public policy areas like health.

Another frequently quoted definition is that from the US Institute of Medicine. It appeared in the same year as Acheson's – 1988 – and is very similar, although there are some differences, including no mention of disease. However, the differences are greater when set alongside Wanless's definition in that the IOM definition asserts that public health is emphatically about community-wide concerns and not those of individuals. The IOM defined public health as fulfilling society's interest in assuring conditions in which people can be healthy. Public health is distinguished from health care by its focus on community wide concerns – the public interest – rather than the health interests of particular individuals or groups. Its aim is to generate organised community effort to address public concerns about health by applying scientific and technological change.

(Institute of Medicine 1988: 1)

Following the Acheson definition more closely, the Department of Health in Australia interprets public health as 'the organised response by society to protect and promote health and to prevent illness, injury and disability' (Population Health Division 1999: 1).

What these and other definitions all share is a consensus favouring the idea of public health as an outcome of organized social and political effort to improve the health gain of communities and groups.

Traditionally, public health has maintained close links with medicine, although notions like the 'new public health' or 'wider public health' have been employed to suggest that the actions of many other professions and organizations have as much influence – and in some cases possibly more – on health improvement than an exclusively medical model of public health or a public health function exclusively centred on health care services. The proximity of public health to medicine and health care remains an uncomfortable one in respect of public health interventions aimed at tackling the social determinants of health, largely because in practice public health is repeatedly overshadowed by more urgent issues arising from the acute health care sector, regardless of the policy rhetoric. In Wanless's words: 'in spite of numerous policy initiatives being directed towards public health, they have not resulted in a rebalancing of policy away from health care' (Wanless 2004: 38).

Some observers regard the close link with medicine as inherently problematic and a handicap that has served to hold back the development of a truly multidisciplinary public health function, especially one that embraces activities beyond the NHS (Evans and Knight 2006). It is not self-evident that this has in fact been a problem. In countries like the US where there has not been a tradition of medical dominance of public health, there remain difficulties in securing an effective public health voice and function, as the IOM's two reports on the future of public health testify. Moreover, some observers believe that public health's position, legitimacy and influence are incorrectly seen to flow from the extent to which it is able successfully to alter the broader determinants of health. In short, it is a deliberate attempt to distinguish the contribution of public health practitioners from that of the powerful clinicians who are dominant in health care (Craig *et al.* 2006).

Another key group of public health practitioners can be found among community nurses. Recent years have seen moves to strengthen the nursing contribution to public health within Europe. With a growing commitment to the public health agenda in many countries, the role of public health nurses is likely to grow. But there remain issues concerning the skills public health nurses need. In a survey conducted in Ireland to establish the scale of public health work and activities undertaken by nurses in the community, especially in the wider sense of public health, when it came to knowledge and skills respondents felt these related primarily to one-to-one or small group interactions within individuals and families. They did not judge themselves to be competent at undertaking community focused public health activities or engage in the wider political and policy arena for health improvement at population level (Poulton *et al.* 2000: 59–60).

The chief medical officer (CMO) for England suggests three features are unique to public health and distinguish it from clinical work (Department of Health 2006). First, staffing levels have remained static and continue to lag behind increases in consultant staff with the result that the public health voice among professional colleagues has become diluted. Second, public health departments since 1974 have been subjected to successive reorganization in a way that has not affected a consultant physician or surgeon. The result has been poor morale, constant 'navel gazing' and a loss of professional skills. Third, although improvements in population health are effective and valuable, the benefits are often long term and not clearly related to individuals. Unlike acute care interventions, they are not immediately visible and those affected by them may be unaware of having avoided illness or premature death. It remains a constant struggle in the allocation of resources to ensure that prevention is not wholly driven out by intervention.

The three domains

Perhaps part of the problem facing public health lies in the sheer breadth and complexity of the function itself. The determinants of health are multiple and complex and, as Figure 2.1 shows, include individuals and their lifestyles at one extreme and the global ecosystem at the other. Indeed, issues around public health and sustainability are increasingly seen as part of the same agenda rather than forming separate agendas. For example, getting people to change their mode of travel from cars to cycling or walking is not only good for the environment and global warming but will also have direct benefits for physical and mental health.

The Faculty of Public Health has identified three domains of public health as follows:

- health protection;
- health improvement;
- health service quality improvement.

The health protection domain embraces the prevention and control of infectious diseases; responding to emergencies, including those resulting from chemicals and poisons, radiation, as well as bioterrorism; dealing with environmental health hazards.

Determinants of Health

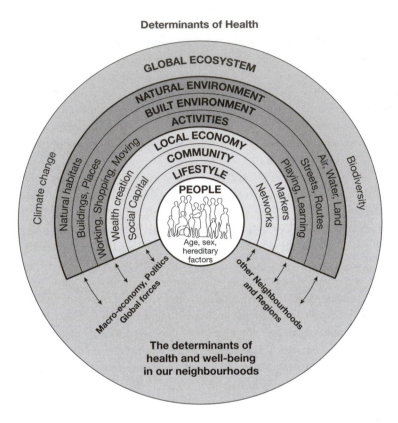

Figure 2.1 Determinants of health (Dahlgren and Whitehead 1991)

The health improvement domain embraces tackling inequalities; working with partners in the NHS and in other sectors such as education, housing, and workplaces; engaging with structural determinants as well as working with individuals and their communities to improve health and prevent disease through adopting healthier lifestyles.

The health service quality improvement domain embraces promoting clinical effectiveness through evidence based practice, service planning and priority-setting, audit and evaluation; supporting clinical governance.

As has been pointed out, the origins of the domains 'lie in the historic importance of the control of communicable disease, health education and the role of hospital and community services over the past 150 years' (Griffiths *et al.* 2005: 910). Conceptualizing the breadth of public health within the framework of three domains of practice is intended to make the management task more manageable. The three domains are not separate entities but overlap and are interdependent. The domains, it is suggested, are not specific to public health practice in England but can be used in any country and public health system (Griffiths *et al.* 2005). In any particular health problem, such as teenage pregnancy or alcohol abuse, the three domains can help both to frame the actions needed and those who need to be engaged in constructing the public health response to the perceived problem. They can also be employed to understand the skill mix needed by those delivering services.

Each of these domains alone entails a sizeable remit involving a different and varied mix of skills and experience. If, for instance, health promotion is unpacked then it demands an exceptional range of competencies, including building cross-government policy and joined-up management, working in partnership with a diverse range of agencies and professionals, and strengthening community action.

Combining the tasks under a single manager or directorate has proved to be a major feat and may go some way towards explaining why managing public health is regarded as especially complex and a task for which few practitioners are well equipped. At the same time, the view commonly heard is that the public health function operates best when the three core activities of service development, health improvement and health protection are undertaken in an integrated manner. However, even those who advocate such a view agree on the need to draw some boundaries around what 'service development' constitutes to avoid a situation where it becomes a 'catch-all' for public health staff to become overly drawn into operational issues that are the responsibility of others (Department of Health, Social Services and Public Safety 2004).

In this book we are primarily concerned with the second and third domains – health improvement, and health service quality improvement. These lie at the heart of policy initiatives intended to improve population health and reduce health inequalities. They also present the greatest challenge in terms of developing appropriate management and leadership skills. We return to these matters in subsequent chapters.

Although the Faculty's three domains have been widely adopted, there are other typologies describing the public health function. Notable among these is Holman's typology of public health movements:

- health protection;
- preventive medicine;
- health education;
- healthy public policy;
- community empowerment.

Unlike the Faculty's domains, Holman's typology is much more specific about the focus of health services, which is on preventive medicine, and also usefully expands the health improvement domain by specifying a range of dimensions (Holman 1992). Otherwise there is considerable overlap between the domains and the typology. The fourth and fifth types are relevant in the context of this book's particular focus.

33

In the UK until 1974, public health practitioners were located in local government – an arrangement that many regarded as more appropriate for the pursuit of the health of a population than a place in the NHS, which was dominated by clinicians and the service needs of individual patients. But the first major reorganization of the NHS in 1974 saw public health, or community medicine as it was then called, move from local government to the NHS where the key tensions between health care and health came to the surface. They were inevitable under an arrangement whereby the management and leadership of public health resided with the health care system whose leaders had little understanding or knowledge of public health and often no interest in it. The hope was that the new speciality would take its rightful place alongside general practice and hospital medicine and compete for resources on equal terms. But things turned out rather differently and the legacy of that reorganization in 1974 remains alive in contemporary debates about the public health function. Part of the problem lies in a perception of the NHS as a national *sickness* service and not a national *health* service.

Even within the NHS it has proved difficult to develop public health in those sectors or professions who might reasonably be expected to support such a develop-ment, notably in primary care. With few exceptions, primary care as it has developed has failed to transform itself from primary medical to primary health care (Peckham and Exworthy 2003). Taylor *et al.* (1998) have identified a number of barriers to effective public health activity, including:

- lack of a 'shared' language – that is, shared definitions of public health between primary care practitioners and other stakeholders, including members of the community;
- poor understanding of collaborative working both within primary health care teams and between GPs and other agencies;
- the dominance of a medical model of primary care with its emphasis on general practice, and medically dominated organization and values;
- poor understanding of the key principles of public health among primary care professionals.

In their work with primary care organizations, Meads *et al.* (1999) identified a number of organizational barriers to developing public health in primary care. In particular, there was a lack of a public health perspective and a consequential absence of public health skills and organizational capacity to work in partnerships with local authorities and others.

While some observers regret such a state of affairs, others believe that the NHS's core business is to treat sickness and ill-health, and that the focus on health should lie elsewhere. Elson, for example, does not view such thinking as an attack on the 'existence or competence' of the NHS (Elson 2004). After all, there is strong public support for services that address the concerns of people who are ill so the medical dominance within the NHS is not at all surprising. But, as Elson also notes, to give equal weight to the public health agenda within an ill-health-dominated service presents real difficulties. What is needed, in his opinion, is a reawakening of a sense of responsibility on the part of local government 'to make the promotion of the public's health a mainstream part of public policy once more' (Elson 2004: 44). Why a reawakening? For Elson (and others) the reasons are simple enough. With the arrival of the NHS, local government gave up its traditional responsibilities for this area of public service, an effect compounded by the transfer of formal public health responsibilities from local government to the NHS in 1974. From then on, anything to do with health was regarded as 'an NHS responsibility'.

The categorization of the public health workforce in the CMO's review (see pp. 37–38) into three broad groupings reinforces, however unintentionally, the somewhat peripheral role accorded local government. Whereas the 'formal' public health workforce comprises public health specialists and practitioners who are firmly embedded in the NHS and who form distinct professional groups, the third category – the wider public health workforce – is no more than an amorphous catch-all grouping to include virtually every other profession whose activities may in some way impact on the public's health. Indeed, assuming a broad definition of health, it is hard to conceive of who might be *excluded* from such an all-embracing term.

But an ongoing struggle persists in local government over its public health role. Gaining wider acceptance for public health as a core part of local government is seen as key to wresting responsibility away from the NHS where public health has a habit of being subsumed within a model that focuses on sickness and ill health (Elson 2004).

These debates and concerns were revisited in the House of Commons Health Committee's 2000–2001 inquiry into public health (House of Commons Health Committee 2001). While a few of the Committee's members, including its then chair, were sympathetic to the notion of returning public health to local government, it was persuaded by the weight of written and oral evidence that the issues were not primarily ones of organizational structure or where functions were located but had much more to do with effective leadership, political will, and a genuine commitment to partnership working.

Nevertheless, there remain tensions and an underlying sense that as long as the lead responsibility for public health remains with the NHS then, in the words of the Health Committee, 'it runs the risk of trailing well behind fix and mend medical services' (House of Commons Health Committee 2001: paragraph 47). Yet, as many commentators, including Wanless, have argued, the NHS, whilst a potentially major contributor, is only one element of the public health delivery system. An essential element, in Wanless's view, is the 'recognition that the greatest contribution to public health is made by individuals in the "wider" public health workforce, many of whom have job titles that do not mention public health, or even health' (Wanless, 2004: 70).

It has been claimed that intersectoral action is necessary at all stages of policy formulation and implementation in respect of chronic disease, as the major determinants lie outside the health sector (Epping-Jordan *et al.* 2005).

Part of the dilemma facing public health may be an image problem arising from the very term 'public health'. Evidence submitted to the House of Commons Health Committee's inquiry into public health bears this out. One organization claimed the term was restrictive and inhibited the broader agenda of the health of the public and the quality of life lived rather than the absence of illness. Public health constitutes a broad church and a new term is needed, like that of the health of the people, to denote this. Certainly the term 'public health' creates problems for organizations like local authorities, which regard it as solely a health care responsibility. Local government prefers a term like 'well-being' or 'social responsibility' to describe its contribution to improved health.

But apart from difficulties around definition and language, there were also deficits in the structure and functioning of public health in the UK as reaffirmed in the CMO's public health function review published at the same time as the Health Committee's report (Department of Health 2001). The function review was undertaken in response to the government's desire to improve the health of the population as a whole, but especially that of the worst-off sections of society. Implementation, it was argued, would not succeed without a strong public health function equipped with the requisite skills and competencies. Doubts had been expressed over whether the function was 'fit for purpose'. Five major themes emerged as essential for a successful public health function:

- a wider understanding of health and well-being;
- better coordination and communication within the public health function;
- effective joined-up working;
- sustained community development and public involvement;
- an increase in capacity and capabilities in the public health function.

The CMO's report was accompanied by well-founded suspicions that it was merely an exercise in 'going through the motions' rather than heralding the start of a significant new phase in the evolution of public health. In particular, was it simply another example of symbolic policy-making and gesture politics from which public health seemed to suffer more than its fair share? The fact that there was considerable delay in its publication suggests the existence of some truth in these assertions. Indeed, had it not been for the Health Committee's pressure for the report to be published it may never have seen the light of day.

Evidence to support this assessment of the function review came a few years later in the Wanless report on public health. In a wide-ranging critique of the failure of public health to deliver despite numerous policy statements, Wanless (2004: 70) concluded that 'developments to strengthen public health capacity need to address both the knowledge and competence of individual members of the workforce, and the capacity of organisations to support and deliver public health activity'. In addition, the Institute of Medicine's report found that a number of systemic problems were evident in explaining the shortcomings of America's public health 'system'. Problems of underfunding, fragmentation, lack of coordination at all levels of government were rife, 'with dire consequences for the public's health' (Institute of Medicine 2003: 26). The report adopted the concept of a public health system to describe a complex network of individuals and organizations that have the potential to play critical roles in creating conditions for health.

As the previous section has shown, a stage has been reached in England (probably less apparent in Wales or Scotland) where the concept of the 'public realm' is being challenged, if not undermined, by business or commercial notions of what constitutes successful governance. The blurring of the public–private boundary in areas like health in the interests of abandoning ideology and supporting what works may, however unwittingly, be making the job of public health and its practitioners increasingly problematic (Jochelson 2005; Hunter 2005; Le Grand and Hunter 2006; Blair 2006).

THE MULTIDISCIPLINARY PUBLIC HEALTH WORKFORCE

As noted earlier, 'a wide range of individuals across a variety of organisations can be considered to have a public health role' (Wanless 2004: 67). The point was also noted in the CMO's report on the public health function, which identified three broad categories of people who contribute to the public health workforce (Department of Health 2001). The categories are as follows:

Specialists: consultants in public health medicine and specialists in public health who work at a strategic or senior management level or at a senior level of scientific expertise to influence the health of the whole population or of a selected community. These professionals have specialist knowledge and skills and their core task is public health. There are currently ten specialist areas of public health practice (see Box 2.1). Each area is divided into knowledge (knows, knows how) and experience (shows how) competences. These underpin the UK Voluntary Register for Public Health Specialists through which consultant-level specialists from any background (that is, not only clinical as previously) can be admitted to the Register. The Register seeks to protect the public through registration but also to enhance the professional standing of the diverse professionals who work in the field of public health.

Public health practitioners: those who spend a major part, or all of their time, in public health practice. These include public health nurses (e.g. health visitors), specialized health promotion staff, community pharmacists, the health protection work of environmental health officers or community development workers. Work has been undertaken in regard to some of these groups as a contribution to public

---

**BOX 2.1   TEN KEY AREAS FOR PUBLIC HEALTH
SPECIALISTS**

1   Surveillance and assessment of the population's health and well-being.
2   Promoting and protecting the population's health and well-being.
3   Developing quality and risk management within an evaluative culture.
4   Collaborative working for health and well-being.
5   Developing health programmes and services and reducing health inequalities.
6   Policy and strategy development and implementation to improve health and
    well-being.
7   Working with and for communities to improve health and well-being.
8   Strategic leadership for health and well-being.
9   Research and development to improve health and well-being.
10 Ethically managing self, people and resources to improve health and well-
    being.

---

health workforce development (see Box 2.2). This has entailed defining roles, functions and development needs of staff and improving their 'fitness for purpose'.

Wider public health: most people, including health care managers, have a role in health improvement and reducing inequalities, although they may not have recognized this. Such a category includes teachers, social care workers, youth workers, local business leaders, transport engineers, town planners, housing officers, regeneration managers, local authority councillors, and so on. As Wanless noted, the wider public health workforce is not easy to define and enumerate. He also argued that the greatest contribution to public health is made by individuals in this category who often do not have 'public health' or even 'health' in their job titles.

The breadth of public health across the three categories suggests that public health is less a speciality with clearly defined boundaries than an arena in which people who would not immediately consider themselves to be public health practitioners apply their skills and expertise to what are essentially public health concerns. Indeed, these people are especially important. While the specialist public health workforce is an essential component of the public health function it is small and 'to achieve greatest impact must engage with and harness the resources of other contributors across all sectors' (Wanless 2004: 70). It is for these reasons that debates continue to rage over how far public health should remain medicalized, and over whether the NHS should retain a lead role for public health or allow this to be transferred to local government. However, regardless of where public health should be located, it is widely acknowledged that the interdisciplinary nature and working of public health is crucial and needs to be established more firmly.

BOX 2.2   THE ROLE OF SPECIALIZED HEALTH PROMOTION STAFF IN IMPROVING HEALTH

A review of the specialized health promotion workforce in primary care trusts and local public health teams was commissioned because of evidence that specialized health promotion had been eroded in recent years due to repeated organizational change and lack of focused and proactive advocacy and development (Department of Health 2006). The discipline had lost confidence in the future. The review team concluded that the knowledge base and experience of over twenty years of specialized health promotion practice needed to be retained and renewed. In particular, the workforce needs

- recognition and advocacy;
- systematic skills and competency development.

Specialized health promotion staff build capacity for the implementation of sustainable public health interventions. They ensure that the processes of delivery are evidence-based.

In particular, such staff

- help people to make and maintain informed health choices by providing information, resources, training and support for the wider public health workforce;
- empower and mobilize local communities for health, including the optimal use of different settings for health promotion (schools, workplace);
- develop health programmes and services, especially to reduce inequalities in health, drawing on the theoretical models and principles of effective health promotion practice.

The review also acknowledged that health promotion expertise, especially in community empowerment and behaviour change, needs to be encouraged within the public health workforce as a whole.

Within the context of multidisciplinary public health, the pride of place accorded public health specialists is the subject of some criticism. It is claimed that significant progress has been made in developing the skills, training and employment opportunities for this group in contrast to the lack of progress made in increasing the capacity and capability among front-line public health practitioners, such as public health nurses and environmental health officers, as well as the 'wider workforce'

(Brocklehurst *et al.* 2005). A major factor for this contrasting progress appears to be 'the more effective and coherent professional and policy leadership which exists for public health specialists than is evident for the other two groups' (Brocklehurst *et al.* 2005: 996). Reinforcing this belief is the continuing absence of the long-promised national public health workforce strategy for England. It is almost certainly the case that its absence may be more keenly felt by the practitioner and wider workforce groups, which together are estimated to account for about 99.63 per cent of the total public health workforce as defined by the CMO's review (Sim *et al.* 2002). As Brocklehurst *et al.* (2005: 996) conclude: 'it is easier to develop a highly specialised workforce in the absence of a coherent national strategy than it is to develop a much larger, and infinitely more diverse, non-specialist one'.

Whatever the alleged imbalance between the three categories comprising the public health workforce, the place of public health specialists remains important. Dalziel (2000) reports on a review of their role by the former Thames region. It demonstrated that a broad range of stakeholders both inside and outside the NHS 'considered the principles and practice of the public health specialist to be central to the health decision making process' (p. 703). Among the skills deemed important for public health specialists, uppermost was the need for technical competence in the surveillance, analysis, synthesis and evaluation of health and health care issues. Another skill was the ability of specialists to develop and facilitate extensive networks both inside and outside the NHS.

However, the review also discovered that the role and purpose of specialists, while valued by those who worked closely with them, was largely invisible to those who had little contact with them. The impression, therefore, was that the specialist had little influence on policy and practice. This suggested the need not only for technically competent specialists but also for those with leadership skills who would be able to influence and persuade at the highest levels. As Dalziel put it:

> Without the subtle skills needed to achieve change in a less than receptive environment, its practitioners will fail, however technically competent. Public health interests would then remain invisible, undervalued and without influence.
>
> (Dalziel 2000: 703)

In particular, the use of skills such as negotiation, political awareness and strategic thinking were deemed especially important.

As noted earlier, there remains a concern that the attention and priority given to the development needs of public health specialists is not present when it comes to public health practitioners or the wider public health. Attempts are being made to remedy the imbalance, such as the North West London public health practitioner training programme, but much more remains to be done (Brocklehurst *et al.* 2005).

At the root of the imbalance between the three categories comprising the public health workforce in England is the issue over the medicalization of public health. In some countries this is no longer an issue – if, indeed, it ever was. Take Australia, for example, where there is no debate – the public health movement is a broad church and its members are all viewed as equal. A similar state of affairs exists in the US. Even in the UK there has been modest progress in achieving a truly multidisciplinary public health, and it is no longer regarded as tenable for public health medicine to dominate. In what is intended to be more than a symbolic gesture, the Faculty of Public Health Medicine has recognized this by dropping 'Medicine' from its title and opening up membership to non-medical candidates. Nevertheless, though these are signs of positive change, the Faculty continues to maintain control over entrants into public health who are not doctors and who choose the voluntary register route. The UK Voluntary Register of Public Health Specialists also closely follows the traditional curriculum of medical public health specialists. And, finally, the very fact that the Faculty remains within the Royal College of Physicians rather belies its true origins and reinforces its medical roots and history.

There is also concern that efforts to promote the multidisciplinary workforce have served to replace one elite (medicine) with another, albeit a slightly enlarged one. Since, as mentioned, not all those who might be doing public health see themselves as having a public health function, then whether the multidisciplinary public health label is sufficient to 'weld a commonality of purpose among these diverse groups is questionable' (Naidoo *et al.* 2003: 81). Trying to impose boundaries round what might be termed 'multidisciplinary public health' risks excluding important disciplines and groups that make a significant contribution to public health. Since many of these already possess relevant skills there seems little sense in reinventing these. Rather, public health should draw on existing expertise and encourage a more flexible skills mix among staff.

Given the wide-ranging nature of the public health task, a wide range of disciplines contribute to public health, including epidemiology, environmental health, disease prevention and health promotion, health information, biology, nursing, medicine, statistics, medical sociology, health psychology, social policy, health economics, and the organization and management of health care.

Of these various disciplines it has been argued that those engaged in public health have not generally been equipped with the requisite management skills in order both to support the case for public health investment and to ensure that agreed plans and proposals are implemented. Indeed, there is a widespread perception that public health, and especially those with a medical background, have been concerned more with knowledge acquisition than with its application to change practice (Hunter and Berman 1997; Nutbeam and Wise 2002). Some consider this to be a reflection of public health's tendency to eschew socio-political action in favour of a misguided adherence to a spurious objectivity in the belief that the public health enterprise is a value-free objective science. As McKinlay and Marceau put it:

> if public health is to be even more successful in the 21st century, it must comprehend the magnitude of the forces against it and the strategies used to engineer its defeat. We all know that our preventive interventions must be appropriate to their sociocultural context, yet we ourselves tend to overlook the socio-political context of the public health enterprise.
>
> (McKinlay and Marceau 1998: 3)

They argue for a willingness on the part of those working in public health to rethink their posture of value-neutrality and objectivity in order to encompass the types of social action and skills needed to combat the social determinants of health.

TOWARDS A PUBLIC HEALTH SYSTEM

The organizational mechanism for achieving the best population health – the public health system – has been defined as encompassing 'activities undertaken within the formal structure of government and the associated efforts of private and voluntary organisations and individuals' (Institute of Medicine 1988: 42). More recently, and building on its 1988 definition, the Institute of Medicine uses the concept of a public health system to describe a complex network of individuals and organizations that have the potential to play critical roles in creating the conditions for health (Institute of Medicine 2003). They can act for health individually, but when they work together towards a health goal they act as a system – a public health system.

Obvious actors in a public health system are:

- governmental public health agencies – national and local;
- health care delivery system;
- academic public health and related health sciences segments of academia;
- communities;
- business and employers;
- media.

In general, nowhere is the public health system sufficiently well integrated to ensure optimal communication, information transfer, and collaboration. Its component parts are also not fully appreciative or aware of their roles and the need to act in concert.

The point about the public health system is that it is not just health departments that play a role in carrying out essential public health functions. As noted above, other sectors of society can contribute by transforming their impacts on the public's health so that they are no longer the result of random and unintentional actions but are the result of informed, strategic, and deliberate efforts to affect health positively.

The health care delivery system, as has also been noted, plays an important role in providing public health and one that for the most part it has failed to deliver on. For example, health care providers can contribute to public health surveillance and assessment of community health status, and they can employ their resources in health promotion and education activities.

By its very definition, the public health system is an example of a complex adaptive system (Plsek and Greenhalgh 2001), and health inequalities are a particular manifestation of the sort of 'wicked issue' that a public health system is intended to confront (see Chapter 3). Health inequalities constitute a wicked issue in that they are imperfectly understood, with solutions that are not clear, and require joint action across a range of services and with the public themselves. The fragmentation of governance at all levels reduces the capacity to identify and respond to these problems, and performance management systems still largely reflect such boundaries.

Inequalities in health occupy a zone of complexity that demands responsiveness, a culture of learning and inquiry, and levels of local innovation. Complex adaptive systems exist where there is no theory of change connecting an action to an outcome. The relationship between what partner agencies do, and progress with a wicked issue such as narrowing the gap in life expectancy or teenage pregnancies between a local district and the national average, is unlikely to be straightforward: it is not a linear or mechanical relationship but one of complexity. This complexity arises from the emergent outcomes of interaction, which are contingent, contextual and difficult to predict in detail (such as doing A will achieve B).

Adaptive systems thinking may be contrasted to more orthodox mechanical thinking. For example, a mechanistic approach to failing to meet a smoking cessation target would be for a primary care organization to increase funding for smoking cessation programmes based on individual counselling services and nicotine replacement therapy. This reflects a linear model of change: more spending on smoking cessation services produces a decline in smokers. However, there is now considerable evidence that the contexts in which smoking rates are highest are where people are coping with worklessness, very low incomes or poor neighbourhood liveability such as dereliction or crime. Higher spending on smoking cessation programmes may have the unintended consequence of widening the gap in smoking rates between people living with these conditions and others who are more motivated to respond to health promotion messages. A more successful strategy may be to focus the resources of the primary care organization and local authority on reducing levels of worklessness and crime in the most deprived areas, creating the conditions in which people consider it worth investing in their future health by giving up smoking.

Plsek (2001) proposes a set of working principles that can inform this kind of adaptive systems thinking that is central to the successful functioning of a public health system:

- create conditions for local innovation and experimentation, and learning from them;
- create forums that share information and make connections between people;
- create simple rules that will promote innovation and development to move the system in the right direction – for example, in health improvement work such a rule could be to avoid actions likely to widen inequalities even if these are likely to improve health for some.

Chapman (2004a, 2004b) adds the following features of 'system practice', contrasting this with a command and control approach:

- ongoing interventions based on learning from what works rather than specifying targets to be met;
- prioritizing overall system performance as judged by end-users and not just by civil servants and ministers;
- policy-making focuses on processes of improvement rather than control;
- other agents and stakeholders are engaged on the basis of listening and co-researching rather than telling and instructing, with responsibility for innovation and improvement widely distributed;
- implementation deliberately fosters innovation and includes evaluation and reflection as part of overall design.

These principles could be used to inform action-learning programmes offered to support knowledge development in public health leadership. One such example is described in Chapter 7.

Issues for a 'fit for purpose' public health system emerged from a regional workshop organized to provide a clear understanding of a robust public health system for the region, to begin to scope its shape, and to highlight the issues that must be addressed (Ellis 2005) (see Box 2.3). Subsequent chapters go more deeply into selected issues to ensure that such a system can be made to succeed.

The workshop concluded with a set of key messages to government (see Box 2.4).

STRENGHENING PUBLIC HEALTH CAPACITY AND CAPABILITY

For some time it has been acknowledged that equipping the public health workforce so that it can deliver the government's strategy must be a priority. The CMO's public health function review identified a number of strands, including increasing workforce capacity, strengthening multidisciplinary public health, strengthening capabilities, and leadership and management development (Department of Health 2001). It is the last of these that is the subject of this book.

BOX 2.3 ISSUES FOR A 'FIT FOR PURPOSE' PUBLIC HEALTH SYSTEM

- The overall public health system needs to be mapped and described: which organizations are part of it, and what each is required to contribute to improve and protect health. An organization's contribution to public health should not be optional. Organizations with a public health obligation should be held accountable for its delivery.

- Organizational boundaries can be an obstacle to delivery – all relevant organizations should have a duty of partnership and recognize that the public health system will become network driven, with people contributing from all levels. The workforce must be liberated from its 'silos' to enable cross-skilling and provide public health input where the people who need it are located. Public health networks in the region have made a significant contribution to joint working.

- There is too much fragmentation in public health governance between district and regional levels and across different agencies. A more coherent and robust accountability structure is required.

- The subsidiarity principle should apply; namely, that the delivery of public health goals should be undertaken locally wherever possible, and be the responsibility of a jointly accountable director of public health, accountable to the local authority and NHS. Higher tier (e.g. regional) responsibility should be reserved for rare incidents and scarce expertise and for developing strategic frameworks informed by those responsible for local delivery.

- The rate and number of innovative schemes is unsustainable, especially when they are subject to short-term funding and fail to get mainstreamed, even when effective. More work needs to be put into: (a) mainstreaming innovations that work by using real-time research and development that is both relevant and timely in meeting public health goals, and (b) acting on the evidence where appropriate.

- Greater health literacy is called for, as recommended by Wanless in his second report (Wanless 2004); people need to be engaged in their health and understand what contributes to, and damages, it. If people are more health literate, this will act as a form of advocacy and help foster the creation of 'tipping points' whereby pressure is put on government to act in the interests of the public good.

- Employers are a key platform for strengthening health literacy among the workforce, and this is in keeping with the healthy-settings approach advocated in the 1999 public health white paper (Secretary of State for Health 1999). Some 49 per cent of the region's gross domestic product is spent in the public sector – this should be an 'engine' for action on public health. The IT strategy,

45

Connecting for Health, could be an effective tool to engage staff and the public on health literacy.

■ Intelligence needs analysing at a higher level of aggregation, but results should be accessible locally. By 2010 there will be a diversity of providers. Commissioning for health and health care will need an effective contribution from public health. All parts of a public health delivery system should be obliged to collect quality information so it can be analysed and acted upon.

■ Vertical integration of the public health system is needed in respect of (a) shared information systems; (b) shared policy objectives at each level; and (c) high quality R&D.

BOX 2.4 MESSAGES TO GOVERNMENT

■ It is imperative that a coherent public health system is described that has clear accountabilities. Good public health should be in the vanguard of a modernizing policy thrust that aims to improve health.

■ The government's health inequality target on life expectancy nationally is unlikely to be met if the region does not achieve the level of change required, such is the degree of inequality within the region.

■ Recognize the potential for local government as a key driver for public health and well-being working in partnership with the NHS. To this end, joint public health appointments are a means of ensuring effective public health action.

■ The NHS and other sector providers will need effective regulation with regard to their public health roles.

■ Use the commissioning regime to commission health gain. Primary care organizations and general practices will need to commission programmes that improve and protect health whilst tackling inequality.

■ Put performance management of prevention centre stage.

■ Fewer initiatives, more follow-through of what's already being planned and delivered – use local area agreements and local strategic partnerships to full effect.

■ Act on the public health evidence that already exists and develop the R&D strategy to encompass public health research

Under strengthening capabilities, the CMO's review recommended that 'a public health "mindset" should be systematically developed in senior NHS and local authority managers and a range of other professionals in the public sector' (Department of Health 2001: 28). The review also wanted priority attention to be given to strengthening implementation skills in the public health workforce, especially in respect of leadership and advocacy for public health programmes, and skills at working in partnership across sectors and in managing change. These were in addition to technical skills in the areas of epidemiology, needs assessment, critical appraisal and using research evidence.

Despite what were seen to be entirely reasonable and overdue recommendations to improve the capacity and capability of the public health workforce, progress has fallen short of the expectations raised by the review. Perhaps it reflected in part the tendency for public health to be marginalized when it comes to training and development, or a failure to invest sufficiently in those skills where significant deficits were clearly evident, including leadership and management. These were picked up by Derek Wanless in his 2004 review of public health (Wanless 2004). Echoing the CMO's review, he recommended a strategic plan at national level be produced to implement a coordinated approach to developing the public health workforce. No such plan has yet emerged.

Ensuring delivery was the principal theme of the English public health white paper published in 2004, *Choosing health* (Secretary of State for Health 2004). It sought to achieve this through various means, but notably by aligning planning and performance assessment.

However, what remains problematic in the public health workforce's skill mix is an absence of appropriate development opportunities in respect of leadership and management to ensure that health policy priorities that extend beyond curative medicine receive adequate support and a chance of succeeding. In keeping with the theme of the book, subsequent chapters will go into more detail about the developments needed to equip public health practitioners with the requisite change management skills needed to deliver public health activity. Chapter 7 presents as a case study a leadership for a health improvement programme that seeks to tackle many of the issues and deficits reviewed here.

Before leaving the policy and practice context of public health and turning to more specific concerns around the needs of those charged with its management, it needs to be stressed that no amount of training and development investment, no matter how relevant or appropriate, will compensate for an absence of a true sense of purpose and ambition. The recent history of public health is essentially a negative one – a story littered with false hopes and promises and a failure to deliver. How often has it been said that public health is at a crossroads, or that it faces another false dawn? There is a deep-seated 'crisis' in the function that needs to be confronted before attempts to strengthen its capacity and capability can succeed.

The 'crisis' in public health

Writing about the crisis of public health well over a decade ago, Julio Frenk, a public health academic who is Mexico's health minister, noted that public health has historically been one of the 'vital forces leading to collective action for health and wellbeing'. However, 'the widespread impression exists today . . . that this leading role has been weakening and that public health is experiencing a severe identity crisis, as well as a crisis of organisation and accomplishment' (Frenk, 1992: 68). Such a crisis is evident in many countries and stems broadly from the same causes that have been alluded to above. The paradox is that at precisely the time when the challenges facing the public's health, whether it is obesity, alcohol consumption, drug misuse, sexual health, narrowing the health gap between social groups, and so on, demand healthy public policy, governments seem to be retreating from their responsibilities claiming that it is all too difficult and that change can only be forthcoming through individuals acting as consumers and expressing their desires in the marketplace. Where this leaves public health poses a dilemma, especially when much public health practice in the UK is already systemically weakened by being bound up with the fate of the NHS (Berridge 1999; Hunter 2003). One way forward would be for the public health community to exercise more political leverage and advocate for what it believes in, including encouraging local government to assume a stronger leadership role as favoured by Elson (2004).

But the challenge goes further and is succinctly expressed by the Institute of Medicine in its report on the future of the public's health: 'No single individual or group can assure the conditions needed for health. Meaningful protection and assurance of the population's health require communal effort' (Institute of Medicine, 2003: 22). There are limits to markets and to viewing individuals as consumers exercising unfettered choice.

If there is puzzlement and disagreement over what the public health function embraces, who should lead it, whether the term is sufficiently all-embracing, and over what the public realm means in an age of consumers, choice and markets, then there is also uncertainty over who practises public health and call themselves public health practitioners.

In a discussion paper on public management and the essential public health functions (by which it includes disease surveillance, health education, monitoring and evaluation, workforce development, enforcement of public health laws, public health research, and health policy development), the World Bank regards such functions as public goods (Khaleghian and Gupta 2004). Policy-makers in developed countries may wish to take note and heed the Bank's advice. By public goods, the report's authors mean that they are non-rival and non-exclusionary and exist for the benefit of the whole population. In contrast, private goods are both rival and exclusionary. For this reason, the authors argue that public health functions are more akin to other core government functions, such as revenue collection and maintaining law and order, and should be subjected to similar principles for their management. They also acknowledge the extent of market failures in the health sector, particularly for public health functions. Although their paper is aimed at developing countries, its arguments and conclusions are also relevant for developed countries struggling with the challenges posed by rising levels of obesity, alcohol consumption and sexually transmitted infections. Other key lessons from the review of public health management and essential public health functions (EPHFs) are:

- co-payments or user fees are not an option for the EPHFs because of their public goods characteristics;
- promoting competition among agencies responsible for public health functions does not improve efficiency; on the contrary, it impedes collaboration and technical assistance and can therefore compromise the effectiveness of activities such as surveillance and health promotion; significantly in the context of health system reforms in the UK and many other countries, the authors assert that reforms that rely on provider competition (e.g. purchaser–provider splits) are not applicable to EPHFs;
- for EPHFs where measurement is complex and expensive and requires strong information systems, contracting imposes transaction and monitoring costs that make efficiency gains unlikely and reduce effectiveness
- provider incentives are complex and difficult to design for the EPHFs and cannot be simply transferred from the experience with curative care; also, incentives should be team- or network-based rather than individualized and should not neglect the role of non-financial benefits.

CONCLUSION

Given the concerns and findings reported in this chapter, the case for seeing public health in a different light from other public services is a persuasive one. However, as the review of the policy context in Chapter 1 demonstrated, it has not prevented public health from becoming entangled in the health system reforms underway in many countries, with their strong market-style ethos and direction. The neo-liberal thrust of public policy in many countries has not allowed public health to escape or be treated differently. The cyclical struggle between regarding public health as a collective concern on the part of society, or a personal concern on the part of the individual continues (Berridge 1999). Just as in the 1960s, when public health issues underwent a shift away from environmentalism and towards a greater degree of individual responsibility for the maintenance of health, so some 50 years later in 2006 there is a renewed emphasis on the role of the individual.

Little wonder, then, that public health seems to find itself forever in a state of 'crisis' when its very purpose is contested, and when those who comprise its workforce are sometimes unclear what their public health role is. The next chapter attempts to clarify the nature of that task by exploring the relationship of public health with management.

DISCUSSION QUESTIONS

1   Are the commonly used definitions of public health appropriate and 'fit for purpose', given the changes in society and the changing nature of the public realm?
2   Is there a risk of the public health function becoming so broad and diverse that for it to be managed through a single person, albeit supported by a team, presents a particularly (and possibly unnecessarily) complex challenge?
3   Does each of the three domains in public health require the same approach in terms of their organization and management?
4   Is the concept of the public health system useful for thinking about the public health function and what needs to happen at different levels of government and organization?
5   Is the 'crisis' in public health arising from concerns about its lack of achievement, and when the notion of what constitutes the public realm is undergoing reassessment, responsible for a growing sense of unease in the workforce – or might it trigger helpful and possibly overdue changes in the way public health practitioners conceive of their role?

REFERENCES

Acheson, D. (1988) *Public health in England*. Cmnd 289. London: HMSO.

Beaglehole, R. and Bonita, R. (1997) *Public health at the crossroads*. Cambridge: Cambridge University Press.

Berridge, V. (1999) *Health and society in Britain since 1939*. Cambridge: Cambridge University Press.

Blair, T. (2006) Speech on healthy living, 26 July. <www.number10.gov.uk/output/Page9921.asp>.

Brocklehurst, N., Hook, G., Bond, M. and Goodwin, S. (2005) Developing the public health practitioner work force in England: lessons from theory and practice. *Public Health*, 119(11): 995–1002.

Chapman, J. (2004a) *System failure: why governments must learn to think differently*, 2nd edition. London: Demos.

Chapman, J. (2004b) Thinking out of the machine, in T. Bentley and J. Wilsdon (eds) *The adaptive state: strategies for personalising the public realm*. London: Demos.

Craig, N., Wright, B., Hanlon, P. and Galbraith, S. (2006) Does health care improve health? *Journal of Health Services Research and Policy*, 11(1): 1–2.

Dahlgren, G. and Whitehead, M. (1991) *Policies and strategies to promote social equity in health*. Stockholm: Institute of Futures Studies.

Dalziel, M. (2000) Leadership for health. How can we ensure that the values and principles of public health become central to health and social policy? *Journal of Epidemiology & Community Health*, 43(9): 703–704.

Department of Health (2001) *The report of the chief medical officer's project to strengthen the public health function*. London: Department of Health.

Department of Health (2006) *Shaping the future of public health: promoting health in the NHS*. Project Report. The role of specialized health promotion staff in improving health. London: Department of Health.

Department of Health, Social Services and Public Safety (2004) *Public health function review in Northern Ireland*. Belfast: DHSS & PS.

Ellis, T. (2005) *Regional public health systems event workshop*. Manchester: Cheshire and Merseyside Public Health Network.

Elson, T. (2004) Why public health must become a core part of council agendas, in K. Skinner, (ed.) *Community leadership and public health: the role of local authorities*. London: Smith Institute, pp. 39–48.

Epping-Jordan, J.A., Galea, G., Tukuitonga, C. and Beaglehole, R. (2005) Preventing chronic diseases: taking stepwise action, *The Lancet*, 5 October.

Evans, D. and Knight, T. (eds) (2006) *'There was no plan!' – the origins and development of multidisciplinary public health in the UK*. Report of witness seminar held at the University of the West of England on 7 November 2005.

Frenk, J. (1992) The new public health, in Pan American Health Organization, *The crisis of public health: reflections for debate*. Washington: PAHO/WHO, pp. 68–85.

Griffiths, S., Jewell, T. and Donnelly, P. (2005) Public health in practice: the three domains of public health. *Public Health*, 119: 907–913.

Holman, J. (1992) Something old, something new: perspectives on five 'new' public health movements. *Health Promotion Journal of Australia*, 2(3): 4–11.

House of Commons Health Committee (2001) *Public health. Second report. Volume 1: Report and proceedings of the committee*. Session 2000–01. HC30-I. London: HMSO.

Hunter, D.J. (2003) *Public health policy*, Cambridge: Polity.

Hunter, D.J. (2005) Choosing or losing health? *Journal of Epidemiology & Community Health*, 59(12): 1010–1013.

51

Hunter, D.J. and Berman, P.C. (1997) Public health management: time for a new start? *European Journal of Public Health*, 7(3): 345–349.

Institute of Medicine (1988) *The future of public health.* Washington: National Academies Press.

Institute of Medicine (2003) *The future of the public's health in the 21st century.* Washington: National Academies Press.

Jochelson, K. (2005) *Nanny or steward? The role of government in public health.* London: King's Fund.

Khaleghian, P. and Gupta, M.D. (2004) *Public management and the essential public health functions.* World Bank Policy Research Working Paper 3220. Washington: World Bank.

Le Grand, J. and Hunter, D.J. (2006) Debate: choice and competition in the British National Health Service, *Eurohealth*, 12(1): 1–3.

McKinlay, J.B. and Marceau, L.D. (1998) *Value for money in the battle for the public health.* Boston: New England Research Institutes.

Meads, G., Killoran, A., Ashcroft, J. and Cornish, Y. (1999) *Mixing oil and water: how can primary care organisations improve health as well as deliver effective health care?* London: Health Education Authority.

Naidoo, J., Orme, J. and Barrett, G. (2003) Capacity and capability in public health, in J. Orme, J. Powell, P. Taylor, T. Harrison and M. Grey (eds) *Public health for the 21st century: new perspectives on policy, participation and practice.* Maidenhead: Open University Press.

Nutbeam, D. and Wise, M. (2002) Structures and strategies for public health intervention, in: R. Detels, J. McEwen, R. Beaglehole and H. Tanaka (eds) *Oxford textbook of public health.* Volume 3: *The practice of public health,* 4th edition. Oxford: Oxford University Press, pp. 1873–1888.

Peckham, S. and Exworthy, M. (2003) *Primary care in the UK: policy, organisation and management.* Basingstoke: Palgrave Macmillan.

Plsek, P. (2001) Redesigning health care with insights from the science of complex adaptive systems, in Institute of Medicine, *Crossing the quality chasm: a new health system for the 21st century.* Washington: National Academics Press.

Plsek, P.E. and Greenhalgh, T. (2001) The challenge of complexity in health care. *British Medical Journal*, 323: 625–628.

Population Health Division (1999) *An overview of health status, health care and public health in Australia.* Occasional Papers Series No. 5. Canberra: Department of Health and Aged Care.

Poulton, B., Mason, C., McKenna, H., Lynch, C. and Keeney, S. (2000) *The Contribution of nurses, midwives and health visitors to the public health agenda.* Belfast: Department of Health, Social Services & Public Safety.

Secretary of State for Health (1999) *Saving lives: our healthier nation.* Cm 4386. London: HMSO.

Secretary of State for Health (2004) *Choosing health: making healthier choices easier.* Cm 6374. London: HMSO.

Sim, F., Schiller, G. and Walters, R. (2002) *Public health workforce planning for London. Mapping the public health function in London.* A report to the DHSC London. London: Department of Health.

Taylor, P., Peckham, S. and Turton, P. (1998) *A public health model of primary care: from concept to reality.* Birmingham: Public Health Alliance.

Wanless, D. (2004) *Securing good health for the whole population.* Final Report. London: HM Treasury.

Chapter 3

Exploring managing for health

David J. Hunter

KEY POINTS OF THIS CHAPTER

- The relationship between management and public health is an uneasy and ambivalent one
- Different models of management can be identified, and locating which is the most appropriate for public health is an important first step
- Management and medicine have too often been at odds instead of working together; this has affected the public health function and its approach to management
- Much New Public Management thinking is inappropriate for public health because it is mechanistic, hierarchical and overly prescriptive and fails to acknowledge the complexities of public health
- A new managerial paradigm embracing notions of complexity is required
- The notion of public health management, based on combining knowledge with action, may offer a way forward
- Public health managers require support in change management and organization development

INTRODUCTION

Within the health sector there has been a global revolution in the organization of health services. Management has been held up as the principal instrument through which the supply-side objectives of the various reforms can be achieved, as well as those that seek to shift the emphasis in health policy away from an exclusive concentration on health services and towards the notion of health in its wider sense.

The relationship between management and public health has been a long-standing and, at times, difficult one. In modern health care systems, public health needs management more than ever, but this reliance, not always recognized or accepted, often causes offence or a feeling of unease because it is regarded in some quarters as leading to unacceptable compromise in respect of the scientific knowledge-based bedrock of the speciality of public health medicine. There is no equivalent science of managing since management is contingent upon particular circumstances and contexts and has no universal application (Goodwin 2006). Hardly surprising, therefore, that considerable ambivalence exists in the relationship between public health and management.

The tension set up by the public health medicine ethos of rational scientific inquiry on the one hand and the management ethos of making change happen on the other can be entirely healthy and creative since the excesses of one can be tempered by those of the other. For example, sometimes management is about achieving change for which there exists no (or incomplete) evidence that it is the right thing to do or will even work. Conversely, public health specialists have been variously accused of not acting on the results of their scientific inquiries, or of taking too long to complete these when the need for action is pressing, and of being managerially weak or incompetent especially when it comes to the need for political skills in winning support for a particular line of action. The consequence has often been a failure to implement policies or to manage change effectively.

But the relevance of management 'science' for public health can only be established if it is seen to contribute to public health's primary purpose of improving the health of populations. Recent developments in management in many health care systems around the world which have undergone, are undergoing, or can expect to undergo reform create particular difficulties for public health. For most of the past decade or so, with brief interludes, these have centred on market models aimed at improving efficiency through competition and market-style incentives, and directed towards the needs and preferences of individual consumers or users of services rather than the needs of communities or populations. The tension between meeting the needs of populations on the one hand and those of the individual on the other poses a special challenge to public health practitioners and managers charged with the task of finding an acceptable balance between them.

Against this context, this chapter is organized into six sections. It is principally concerned with the relationship between management and public health and with what managing for health might mean for those engaged in the task of health improvement. The first section sets out four world-views or doctrines of management, which provide a framework for the remainder of the discussion in this chapter. The second section examines the notion of management in the context of health care reform and the relationship between management and medicine. The third section considers the particular, and rather difficult, relationship between management and public health. The fourth section suggests the need for a new managerial paradigm to reflect the distinctive requirements and challenges of public health. The notion of public health management is presented and described in the fifth section. The final section reviews the needs of those who practise public health management and what they require in order to be able to function more effectively.

MODELS OF MANAGEMENT

There are four 'world-views', or doctrines, about the management of organizations (Moore 1996). These can assist in understanding the particular circumstances arising from managing medicine and health respectively. The doctrines are:

- *Traditional bureaucracy* – with an emphasis on clear structure, hierarchical chains of command, clear accountability for performance (Taylor 1911).
- *New Public Management* – with an emphasis on making organizations more like firms operating in markets through the introduction of competition to improve performance (Hood 1991).
- *'Japanese' organization model or 'clan'* – 'solidarity' model of organization in which a sense of identity with, and pride in, the organization itself is the main source of motivation.
- *Professionalism* – shares the 'Japanese' model's assumption that people work better when they are trusted and their performance is not closely monitored; the sense of identity is with the profession rather than with the organization, or possibly loyalty to both exists.

The central point about these world-views, or doctrines, is that management is not a purely technical enterprise. Ideas, culture and ideologies make a real difference. Within many health care systems undergoing reform, there has been a shift from models of traditional bureaucracy and professionalism to a model of new public management where the emphasis is on encouraging public bureaucracies to mimic some of the alleged successful features of private sector management practices. These include government and public services steering more and rowing less, being mission-driven rather than rule bound, and being more responsive to the customer and to quality (Osborne and Gaebler 1993). But there are limits to the utility of such managerial models to essentially professional types of work and organization, as subsequent sections show.

MANAGEMENT AND MEDICINE

Biomedical systems operate very differently from complex management systems and are able to subscribe to scientific principles of thought and action, and cause and effect, that, although sometimes applied to management (e.g. as in the notion of scientific management), are rarely valid (Taylor 1911) . Perhaps it is their personalities or their training for this world or both that makes clinicians in general (there are of course always exceptions), including public health specialists, unfit or ill-equipped for a management role, especially of the type studied by Kotter involving paradox, ambiguity and uncertainty (Kotter 1982).

Whereas they may be searching illusively for an understanding of their managerial role rooted in a science of management along the lines of 'Taylorism' and 'scientific management', in fact what is required is a quite different conception of the management task. Unlike medicine, the nature of managerial skills is not clearly established, nor are they standardized to the same extent despite the parallels between clinical systems and business processes and the notion of systematization (Degeling *et al.* 2004). Practitioner-controlled knowledge does not exist in management as it does in medicine. Managerial skills deal with much more variable, contingent and unstable phenomena, which include managerial practices themselves. Management's interdependence with the very realities it seeks to control or influence shapes it.

The history of health care reform globally has been one marked by border skirmishes between managers and professions, notably the medical profession. At the core of the management revolution in health care has been the view that doctors must increasingly accept managerial responsibility as well as be managed themselves by non-medical professional managers. Such developments are more evident in some countries than others, notably the UK, US, Australia and New Zealand. In a nutshell, in these health systems bureaucratic politics have eroded the medical profession's authority. 'Control over health policy has passed from providers and legislators to the health bureaucracy', states one observer (Morone 1993: 731). The managed care movement has evolved to monitor in detail the ways in which physicians operate. What was once deemed specialized knowledge is now subject to protocols, guidelines, and to third-party review. Professional models of organization are progressively being transformed into managerial ones. The micro-management of medical work is in evidence in many health care systems in Europe and beyond. It is occurring through an emphasis on evidence-based medicine and on concepts like clinical governance, which are intended to improve clinicians' performance by encouraging them to manage their work more effectively. Much of the thinking underlying clinical governance includes managerial notions like leadership, creating development plans, clarifying accountability, and so on. These various developments have led to intense debate among sociologists about the extent to which medicine has become 'deprofessionalized' and 'proletarianized' (Hafferty and McKinlay 1993; Hunter 2006). One way of resolving the tension between management and medicine is to engage clinicians in the management task so that they become truly empowered managerially and assume responsibility for their decisions. Many observers would argue that clinicians are *de facto* managers in any case, even if they often seek to deny it, and that it is therefore essential that they take on the management function

(Griffiths 1983). In this way, and through an explicit acknowledgement of their managerial role, 'responsible autonomy' prevails (Degeling *et al.* 2004).

MANAGEMENT AND PUBLIC HEALTH

Those engaged in public health, especially the specialists dedicated to and specifically trained in it, occupy a halfway position between the worlds of management and professionalism. They may therefore be partially exempted from the power play between medicine and management described on pp. 56–58 because they subscribe to a population-based approach to health care and are generally more sympathetic than many of their acute sector clinical colleagues to a managerial perspective on matters like planning and priority-setting. This is despite many public health specialists often feeling inadequately prepared, or equipped, for the management jobs they end up occupying, as was noted in the previous chapter. Public health practitioners, like managers (and vice versa), are usually more concerned about the collective; that is, about the whole population within a locality. The difficulty has been that, until fairly recently, those undergoing training in public health received no more than a very general introduction to management theory and practice and were certainly not prepared for many of the posts that they subsequently occupied, especially at director or board level.

But if the frontier between medicine and management is shifting perceptibly towards managers as a result of successive health system reforms, should this not work to the advantage of public health and those who practise it? Or do public health specialists feel threatened by, and/or oppose, the tighter managerial grip that is evident throughout many health systems on the grounds that it can operate to compromise their professional independence, curtail their freedom as professionals to speak out, and exert inappropriate pressure to produce quick results (Jewell 1999)?

Many of those engaged in public health are ambivalent in their response to these questions. There are clear divisions of opinion between those who believe public health must be an active part of the management system with a place at the top table in order to influence events, and those who consider that public health should remain detached in order to preserve their independence and professional integrity. In practice it is difficult if not impossible to have it both ways, although this is precisely what some practitioners would prefer to see happen.

Part of the dilemma for public health, and its uneasy relationship with management, may lie in the rather crude model of management that many health care systems have had imposed on them, ushered in by politicians who themselves invariably have had little or no managerial experience and are largely ignorant about how big organizations function. Since the closing years of the last century, virtually no area of public policy has escaped the recrudescence of hard-line managerialism, which over the past decade or so has manifested itself in the term 'New Public Management'

(NPM). According to its principal and original exponent, Christopher Hood, NPM 'is one of the most striking international trends in public administration' (Hood 1991: 3). The principal tenets of NPM include a culture of hierarchy, command and control, measurement, and meeting targets (see Box 3.1). Management thinking around notions of complexity science may represent one means by which the tension between bureaucratic and professional modes of management control, respectively, may be resolved, although this requires clinicians to appreciate that simplistic conceptions of management are not all that passes for it. We return to notions of complexity later in this chapter.

There is no single accepted explanation for the considerable and durable appeal of NPM. It would appear at one level to be a response to global socio-economic changes, with their abhorrence of 'statist' and uniform approaches in public policy and a perception that public services seem to be run more for the convenience of those providing them rather than those paying for and using them. Moreover, the World Bank endorsement of NPM thinking has undoubtedly strengthened its grip on countries and enhanced its popularity (World Bank 1993).

While elements of NPM thinking seem entirely appropriate for particular aspects of health and health care activities, some commentators believe that it is misleading to regard it as a generic solution for every management design problem within health systems (Stewart 1998; Hunter 1999). Other management models may be more appropriate in the conduct of professional work. Rather than polarizing these modes of control, which recent waves of health system reforms have tended to do, the issue may in fact be one of finding a new synthesis in which traditional collegiate

---

BOX 3.1 KEY FEATURES OF NEW PUBLIC MANAGEMENT

- ■ Hands-on professional management in the public sector.
- ■ Standard-setting, performance measurement, and target-setting, particularly where professionals are involved.
- ■ Emphasis on output controls linked to resource allocation.
- ■ The disaggregation or 'unbundling' of previously monolithic units into purchaser/provider functions, and the introduction of contracting.
- ■ The shift to competition as the key to cutting costs and raising standards.
- ■ Stress on private sector management style and a move away from the public service ethic.
- ■ Discipline and parsimony in resource use: cost-cutting, doing more with less, controlling workforce demands.

Source: Hood (1991)

forms of professional organization are in fact precisely those needed in order to achieve effective team working and collaboration among a range of diverse skills on the basis that complex problems demand complex solutions.

Arguably, in the midst of these competing notions of what constitutes effective and sound management, public health is at least in part experiencing the crisis of identity and accomplishment to which Frenk drew attention (see Chapter 2) because it has been expected to conform to an inappropriate and mechanistic 'scientific management' model – the 'old' management imported from much, though by no means all, of the business sector, and some of which lingers on under the guise of NPM. Yet public health's roots in a scientific medical model of health and disease may unwittingly have contributed to the dilemma confronting it. Though severely limited in its ability to describe or modify organizational life, scientific management at least resonated with the rational, scientific tradition underpinning public health medicine from which it derived its legitimacy and credibility. Behavioural approaches to management sit uneasily with the scientific tradition. While the 'new' (public) management, with its emphasis on outcomes, may come closer to public health's concerns, its simultaneous focus on markets and individuals as consumers runs counter to public health's values and responsibilities and to the very notion of what it means to be 'public' and to function in the public realm (Marquhand 2005; Choi *et al.* 2005).

A NEW MANAGERIAL PARADIGM

As the previous section has shown, public health has, from time to time, flirted with management and in its innocence has been drawn to an inappropriate model that negates the intrinsic strengths of the speciality itself (Hunter 2002). These strengths are derived from its roots in the profession of medicine. In this profession, and others, collegiate forms of working operate in place of hierarchy and rigid levels of management. In such a context, management is founded on trust whereas the managerialism prevalent in many health services in recent years, and evident in much New Public Management thinking, is founded on distrust. Performance management is centred on providing proof of performance and on individuals and organizations answering for what they fail to do. Concepts like 'chain of command' and 'centralization versus decentralization' are essentially about exercising control.

In contrast to these mechanistic notions, network structures represent a paradigm shift and derive from the flatter, doughnut-configured organizations that emerged in the 1990s. As Handy predicts, 'organisations will be flatter, more flexible and more dispersed' (Handy 1994: 3). More importantly, he continues:

> The old language of management no longer seems appropriate. It never was appropriate in some quarters. Professional organisations, doctors,

architects, lawyers, academics have never used the word manager, except to apply it to the more routine service functions – the office manager, catering manager. The reason was not just a perverse snobbery but an instinctive recognition that professionals have always worked on the principle of the doughnut. This was necessary because every assignment was slightly different, flexibility and discretion had to be built in.

(Handy 1994: 174)

A key theme of the review of the public health function led by the chief medical officer for England was the need to strengthen leadership and management development across the NHS and local government (Department of Health 2001). The review concluded that public health leadership 'requires a facilitative, influencing style that can make use of horizontal networks in addition to vertical "command and control" networks. Advocacy, political skills and commitment are also important' (Department of Health 2001: 32).

The focus on alliance-building across a range of diverse organizations and professions, as well as the public, will make heavy demands on the public health workforce and require well-honed political and managerial skills in addition to the traditional scientific skills associated with public health. It is a particularly difficult synthesis to achieve, not only because of the range of skills required but also because they emanate from two quite distinct paradigms. As implied above, whereas the traditional basis of public health medicine belongs to the positivist, biomedical view of scientific inquiry, the political and managerial skills base comes from an intuitive, contextual orientation grounded in how organizations work in practice. The tradition is sociological and anthropological rather than biomedical. This may help explain why public health specialists often find rational, linear 'scientific management' theories more immediately appealing than theories of a less 'rational' and more behavioural persuasion where uncertainty, complexity, paradox and ambiguity all figure prominently.

Given the rapid pace of change, the revolution in knowledge, and its transmission via the information superhighway, organizational structures that are not extremely adaptable and open to the environment will simply not survive. Flexible, organic structures look set to replace rigid, inflexible bureaucratic structures. Structures, and the management systems operating them, will need to be more transitory and *ad hoc* at all levels – operational, strategic and administrative (Mintzberg 1980).

Network organizations, which function according to the doughnut principle insofar as they possess a central core surrounded by a constellation of project teams that exist for the duration of particular tasks and then get reformed, will survive. Such structures are flexible and fast moving because they can change quickly as the environment changes. They can also better tap external expertise and knowledge rather than attempt to provide it all in-house.

61

Network organizations are not especially new. Writing in the early 1970s about the loss of the stable state and about what might replace it, Schon offered six roles of the network manager all directed towards the design, creation, negotiation and management of networks (Schon 1973: 184–186):

- systems negotiator;
- 'underground' manager – maintains and operates informal networks;
- manoeuvrer – operates on a project basis;
- broker;
- network manager – oversees official networks of activities;
- facilitator.

These roles are difficult and demand high personal credibility for their successful execution. They are often performed by those who exist on the margins or boundaries of organizations – so-called 'boundroids'. The public health management function is perhaps best understood by drawing parallels between the expectations of it and the notion of network management described by Schon, as well as notions based on complex adaptive systems.

Complexity and health

The value of complexity in health systems was acknowledged in the previous chapter. It has received considerable analytic attention in recent years (e.g. Plsek and Greenhalgh 2001; Chapman 2004). A complex adaptive system has been defined as '[a] collection of individual agents with freedom to act in ways that are not always totally predictable, and whose actions are interconnected so that one agent's actions changes the context for other agents' (Plsek and Greenhalgh 2001: 625). An example of such a system is just about any collection of human beings. Some of the properties of complex adaptive systems (CAS) are as follows (Plsek 2006):

- *Adaptable elements*: the elements of the system can change themselves.
- *Simple rules*: complex outcomes can emerge from a few simple rules that are locally applied.
- *Non-linearity*: small changes can have big effects.
- *Emergent behaviour*: continual creativity is a natural state of the system.
- *Not predictable in detail*: forecasting is inherently an inexact, yet boundable, art.
- *Inherent order*: things can be orderly, even without central control.
- *Context and embeddedness*: there are systems within systems, and that matters.
- *Co-evolution*: the system proceeds forward through constant tension and balance.

CAS may be contrasted to NPM type thinking as follows:

■ simple rules and the notion that complex outcomes can emerge from good enough vision, evidence and minimum specifications may be contrasted with always trying to plan and guide things in great detail in a top-down, hierarchical fashion;
■ become comfortable using varying degrees of certainty and agreement instead of fearing that chaos is the only alternative to planning and control;
■ see paradox, tension and seeming impossibilities as constituting perhaps the best opportunities for change, rather than avoiding them and denying their existence;
■ launch many diverse experiments, reflect on what is happening and keep moving in those directions that seem successful instead of trying to figure out the 'one best way';
■ recognize and try to find ways to work with natural networks and natural energy rather than always relying on formal structures and policies.

As Plsek (2006) puts it, existing principles of management and leadership are based on old metaphors that fail to describe adequately or accurately complex situations. The study of CAS provides new metaphors, and within such systems the complex adaptive manager and/or leader

■ manages context and relationships;
■ creates conditions that favour emergence and self-organization;
■ lets go of 'figuring it all out';
■ relies on 'good enough' analysis of the problem and its solution;
■ requires minimum specifications to act rather than prescribing actions in advance.

As noted above, the tension between bureaucratic and professional models of management respectively lies at the core of public health's uneasy relationship with management and often for reasons that have their origins in the concerns that complex adaptive systems seek to confront. Arguably, therefore, it may not be management *per se* that is the problem but rather the type or style of management to which public health may be expected to conform (Hunter 2002; Hunter and Marks 2005). At the same time, notions of management with a behavioural bias can pose problems for a discipline whose origins lie in a scientific, rational model of disease and illness. Of course, public health, as we have insisted, is not the sole preserve of public health medicine specialists, but they have dominated the public health arena for a considerable period of time and enjoy a status and privileges denied others engaged in public health. The important point is the need to acknowledge a public health management role in the first place and then to appreciate which particular notions or types of management might most appropriately fit the task. Some possible models have been reviewed in this section. The next section considers what public health management is in more detail.

PUBLIC HEALTH MANAGEMENT

As has been noted, improving the health of populations is a challenge confronting all countries in both the developed and developing worlds. A renewed emphasis on health has raised the issue of public health's role in this endeavour and on the role of management in achieving better health.

As health care has become more complex a false antithesis has emerged between public health and health services management (Hunter and Berman 1997). Whereas public health specialists have generally looked outwards towards society and the health needs of the population, health services managers have tended to focus inwards on the organization, and particularly on the financially demanding secondary and tertiary care sectors. The shift towards a primary care-led health care delivery system in countries like the UK is forcing a rethink (Secretary of State for Health 2006). At the same time, many public health practitioners believe that they have become over-identified with health care services. Indeed, this dilemma has become more acute with the growing emphasis on clinical governance and evidence-based medicine, all of which appear fairly dependent on public health practitioner involvement (Wylie *et al.* 1999).

Public health management (PHM) involves 'mobilizing society's resources, including the specific resources of the health service sector, to improving the health of populations' (Alderslade and Hunter 1994: 20). PHM embraces a number of features, as displayed in Box 3.2.

PHM is directed towards managing systems based on health outcomes, both at the level of population-based health programmes and at the level of patient care. Above all, PHM is about leadership and managing change. This is often weak and

---

BOX 3.2   DISTINGUISHING FEATURES OF PHM

Public health management
- is multisectoral and professional;
- combines knowledge and action;
- has epidemiology at its core;
- is influential across all health determinants;
- involves public health reporting, leading to health strategy development;
- communicates with politicians, professionals and the public;
- is influential organizationally and financially;
- lies at the heart of the civic society.

poorly organized and provided in training and development programmes. It includes the roles listed in Box 3.3.

The problem of language and correct terminology bedevils all health care systems. But whatever the drawbacks or limitations of the term 'PHM', they should not be allowed to divert attention from its key distinguishing features.

PHM is essentially concerned with action, and with effecting change through working in multisectoral partnerships. It is, above all, about capacity building in order to improve the chances of effective policy implementation. PHM therefore demands particular skills, especially in the fields of change management and leadership. PHM operates at two levels – at a national policy level, and at a sub-national operational level. Each is considered in turn.

BOX 3.3 ROLES OF PHM

- advocacy and management;
- knowledge and action;
- managerial capacity and infrastructure;
- networking to create partnerships across organizations and disciplines;
- broad involvement of people and skills;
- infrastructure and curricula for education;
- evidence-based policy and practice;
- an outcome-based focus;
- a national agenda for health and health services research.

PHM at a national policy level

An issue is whether PHM is able to serve as the instrument required to bring about change and contribute to a realization of policy. It is the weakness of the infrastructure through which policies become translated into action that has contributed to the failure of repeated attempts to shift the policy debate beyond a continuing bias towards a downstream agenda focused on treatment services.

Several countries have sought to shift the policy debate towards an integrated 'whole systems' perspective; namely, Canada, New Zealand, Finland and the UK. Their experiences share a similar outcome – the disconnection between the thrust of policy and the means to achieve it. The result in each country has been frustration at the lack of progress in shifting resources, or even the attention of managers and practitioners, away from health care to health (Glouberman 2000; Department of Health 1998).

Over the past decade or so in many developed countries, tackling the broader health agenda has been a priority to a greater or lesser degree. But, as we saw in Chapter 1, the abiding tension in health policy – namely, that between developing a long-term public health agenda on the one hand and improving rapid access to acute services on the other – persists and has usually found in favour of the immediate, short-term agenda. Of course, improved access to health care services can contribute significantly to health and to an improved quality of life, but it is still often a case of treating symptoms rather than root causes.

What is largely absent from policy-making is any genuine attempt to ensure that a balance is maintained. Both upstream and downstream determinants of health need to be tackled. Economic and social policy need to be mutually reinforcing (Institute of Medicine 2003; Legowski and McKay 2000; Glouberman 2000; Wanless 2002, 2004).

As was noted in Chapter 1, various countries have produced eloquent and ambitious health strategies. The problem lies principally in moving from theory to action, or from rhetoric to reality, since the diagnosis of the problem is well documented and not at issue. Despite gaps in the evidence concerning the gains to be achieved from adopting a more vigorous upstream policy agenda, sufficient evidence exists to make progress (McPherson 2001; Calman 1998). What countries and their health systems appear to lack is a policy instrument or intervention strategy to enable the research findings and evidence to be acted upon. The concept of PHM is an attempt to provide a framework for such an instrument by combining knowledge-based decision-making with the skills to effect change and act on the knowledge acquired.

Key issues for PHM at a strategic policy level are:

- vision;
- political leadership for health;
- central government policy-making approaches that support the vision and provide leadership;
- delivery mechanisms through regions, localities and communities that serve as instruments for implementation.

Each issue is briefly commented upon.

Vision

There is some debate over whether those countries and governments that have sought to shape a vision for public health have retreated from their initial commitment to it. Ensuring effective linkages lies at the heart of the commitment by many governments to 'joined up' policy, but it is proving difficult to secure in practice as many governments acknowledge. In all countries, more might be done to ensure that complementary policies are genuinely coordinated and effectively communicated. For example, there could be more debate about the relationships among policy objectives – which are overarching and which subordinate, how the achievement of one department's objectives depends on, or contributes to, the achievement of another department's objectives. Such a debate would raise quite complex issues, including:

- What is the hierarchy of goals? Is the ultimate goal to do with economic success, social regeneration, sustainable development, quality of life, well-being or health?
- Is health a means to an end?
- How can policy means and ends, and their interaction, be mapped in a way that makes sense to policy-makers, organizations on the ground, professionals and the public?

Political leadership

In considering political leadership of the public health function, there are issues surrounding the role of ministers with a particular responsibility for public health. Whoever occupies such a ministerial role in any government must be able to bring influence to bear across government departments, have backing to be able to create or influence budgets cross-departmentally, and hold other government departments to account (including civil servants). There are arguments for the lead to come from the centre of government in place of a health department where the focus of attention is invariably on health care services.

Central government policy-making approaches

'Joined up' thinking and action – integrated policy-making and delivery – are key 'process' objectives of government policy in many countries. There are various mechanisms for achieving them, including the following:

- cross-departmental coordination units;
- ministers with responsibility for issues such as public health, women, the family, which cut across traditional departmental boundaries;
- initiatives that require cross-governmental commitment, e.g. violence and injuries prevention programmes, teenage pregnancies programmes, tobacco and health regulation programmes;
- common approaches to problems, e.g. targeting resources on area-based initiatives or 'zones';
- health impact assessment of policy proposals;
- efforts to achieve common approaches to improve performance.

67

Many governments acknowledge that a truly joined up approach is some way off, but they resolve to achieve this objective. The dilemma of central government initiatives that affect the same people in local areas, but which are run separately and not linked together, is generalized in most countries. Joined up government has to be supported not by rhetoric or good intentions but by strong incentives and sustained political commitment.

There could be greater urgency in central government, both about establishing health impact assessment of policies and integrating it with impact assessment in other areas (e.g. environmental impact assessment). A commitment to health impact assessment should be viewed as one of the threshold criteria of interdepartmental partnership. The minimum requirement would be that policies should have no negative impact on health, although the expectation should be that they have some positive impact.

There remains a failure to position health in government in many countries. The numerous initiatives to tackle the health agenda, though welcomed, are not joined up. Health departments need to consider how they relate to other government departments and how they can make use of opportunities to advocate the public health interest more energetically.

In the longer term, the public health focus needs to be effectively marketed and communicated. Too often, public health reacts or responds rather than initiates or leads. In most countries there is a question mark over whether there has been an adequate ongoing communications and development strategy for public health policy. This is in contrast to the attention devoted to monitoring trends in hospital waiting lists and delays in accessing health care.

Delivery mechanisms

Effective delivery requires cross-service and cross-agency approaches with horizontal integration at the local, regional, national and international levels and vertical integration of these levels. Improving the quality of practice requires:

- *Information* – evidence of what works and good practice tailored to local needs.
- *Communication* – helping local agencies to see the links between their activity and the national public health framework.
- *Training and capacity development* – taking account of the diversity of organizations, disciplines and professional cultures involved in the new public health.
- *Development of evidence-based standards.*
- *Not necessarily a case of new resources but a better use of what already exists* – it is crucial to bring initiatives into the mainstream, including their funding, since all too often a rash of well-intentioned schemes are subject to short-term funding: 'projectitis' is rife.

- *Community / customer engagement* – people for whom life is tough are not motivated to engage in healthy lifestyles or community schemes for reasons of civic concern or self-articulation. They do have a set of basic material wants that will interest them, including good housing, a clean environment and freedom from crime / drugs.

PHM at a sub-national level

Managing public health in an integrated health system embraces a number of issues, including:

- national policy framework;
- integration or de-integration;
- organizational options;
- management and funding.

Political commitment from the top is essential if a public health agenda is to be advanced beyond fine words. There need to be national goals and objectives as well as clear and explicit policies, strategies and priorities. Funding must be population-needs based.

To achieve integration, a number of conditions need to be met, including:

- adoption of a health outcomes focus;
- security of public health resources;
- competent purchasing;
- provider organization and network;
- political commitment.

New Zealand offers a model through its district health system. Within this, the hospital is intended to become a resource facility – a supply of resources upon which to draw. Primary care is the driver of the delivery system. Services – primary, secondary (including public health) – are all population based.

In the New Zealand model, public health comprises two components: a clinical dimension and a broader conception of public health. Clinical public health is located inside the health care system and linked to primary care, which is the foundation of the system.

More radical thinking in New Zealand, and more recently in the UK, foresees the disaggregation of the hospital as an organization. Clinical services will become population based, rather than institutionally based, with the hospital becoming only the provider of hotel and clinical support services. This could effectively reduce the dominance, and hence power, of the hospital and lead to a more balanced set of district services where there was a real commitment to health improvement.

These arrangements are expected to refocus the integrated provider system on public health outcomes. Public health will therefore become a key component within the set of services being provided by the district health boards. Public health is one of a set of specialized secondary services, each with an interface with primary health care as the foundation service of the district health system.

Regardless of the country and precise configuration of health policy and services, numerous barriers exist to the effective application of a public health management approach, although they are not insuperable. Health care systems tend to suffer from a dysfunctional intermingling of politics and management so that structures and systems emerge that are less than optimal (Blackler 2006). As noted earlier, short-term time horizons for delivering improved health outcomes run counter to changes in the public's health, which often take many years to achieve. Within this overall policy and governmental context, the implications of PHM for those who become managers are considered next.

PUBLIC HEALTH MANAGERS

Public health management is based on twin intellectual approaches – knowledge and action, which go together. In practice, there has been a tension between knowledge and action, with many practitioners in public health focusing on knowledge rather than on action (Nutbeam and Wise 2002). Public health management seeks to integrate the two approaches so that public health knowledge is harnessed to action through the deployment of appropriate management and planning skills. These skills are rooted in an open systems approach to management, drawing on the related notions of negotiated order and network management previously described.

To this end, public health management demands skills other than those commonly to be found in public health. Those working in today's public health function are expected to respond to the multisectoral nature of health problems and serve a variety of agencies. Working in a multisectoral arena to develop healthy alliances is akin to the marginal position desired by network managers and discussed by Schon (1973).

These are heavy and challenging demands requiring well-honed political and managerial skills, in addition to the traditional scientific and epidemiological skills associated with public health. It is a particularly difficult synthesis to achieve, as noted earlier in this chapter – not because of the range of the skills required but because they come from two quite distinct paradigms. The traditional basis of public health medicine belongs to the positivist, biomedical view of scientific inquiry whereas the political and managerial skills base comes from an intuitive, contextual orientation grounded in how organizations work. The tradition is a social science one rather than a biomedical one. This may explain why public health specialists often find 'scientific management' theories more immediately appealing than theories of a less 'rational' and more behavioural persuasion where uncertainty, complexity, paradox and ambiguity figure prominently. The development of health improvement knowledge, tools and techniques offers a synthesis between these two traditions (see Chapter 7).

Within the public health community there is a need for public health physicians, public health specialists and managers to find an intellectual focus for joint working since each group has a vital contribution to make to the superordinate goal of improved health. Failure to find such a focus can only result in further interprofessional rivalry, a lack of coordinated working, and confirmation that those leading public health are not 'fit for purpose'.

Public health management demands knowledge and management skills of the highest order, and these are in short supply. Public health managers must be able to adopt a strategic approach and be able to describe and understand the health experience of populations and analyse the factors affecting health. To achieve change, skills in leadership and political action are necessary. Managers have to operate in a multi-professional, multi-agency environment and be able to achieve multisectoral change.

In taking forward this multisectoral approach, a number of key processes are involved:

- *building alliances and networks with non-health service organizations*: relationships will be based on influence rather than on direction and control;
- *market management*: having a strategic framework based on health improvement, the capacity to work within alliances, possessing good market-relevant information;
- *attention needs to be given to organizational fitness for purpose*: it means moving away from functional departments and towards a blending of skills in task forces and in project-management initiatives – such a team approach will be looser and more fluid than conventional functional departments with their often lengthy hierarchies and multiple layers of management.

Better shared understanding between public health practitioners and managers of health care systems, who occupy two rather distinct camps, might trigger a more productive way of thinking and hasten appropriate action. But for this to happen on a significant scale, public health has to be seen to be everyone's responsibility. Public health cannot remain the preserve of a few practitioners trained in the speciality of public health medicine who are either ignored or who become co-opted into the running of health services, thereby diluting, or even losing sight altogether of their core function. As a former minister for health in England put it, for too long the overarching label 'public health' has served to bundle together functions and occupations in a way that actually marginalizes them from the health service and other health partners (Milburn 2000).

For PHM to become a reality, a new cadre of managers and practitioners is required who share a common core curriculum in their training and development. Without an element of multidisciplinary training it is impossible to foresee any success in bringing together health systems managers and public health practitioners. PHM demands particular skills, especially in respect of change management and leadership. Traditional public health models and training programmes have not seen these as either relevant or important to the speciality of public health. But to be effective, public health managers must possess both public health and management skills. Presently, there is a skills deficit.

These matters have clear implications for the training and development of public health leaders, a subject to which we will return in Chapter 7. However, from available evidence derived from experience and practice, it is probable that very few health service managers are equipped to operate in the way indicated, either as public health managers or as health service managers working within a strategic public health framework.

As Chapter 1 demonstrated, the political and policy context in which public health and those doing it find themselves is both complex and dynamic and often highly political. Expectations are running high and yet there are few role models available to those engaged in public health to help bring about the change required on the necessary scale. Certainly in the UK, but elsewhere, too, public health managers will be working in new structures and unfamiliar contexts. They will be charged with helping to make their organizations public health organizations, and this will demand a combination of new skills and performing some existing ones more smartly. Vital tools to assist them in their endeavour, and to find solutions that will work, include change management and organization development.

Change management

The literature on change management (CM) is large. In their review of organizational change, Iles and Sutherland (2001) claim that

- it contains contributions from several academic disciplines, including psychology, sociology, business policy, social policy and others;
- its boundaries can be set differently according to the definition of CM employed;
- it contains evidence, examples and illustrations generated in a wide variety of organizations and from a diverse range of methodologies with varying degrees of rigour;
- some material is not readily accessible to non-specialists and does not readily lend itself to cumulative review;
- the concepts included within it range in scale from whole academic schools through methodologies to single tools.

A major problem in the CM field is the prevalence of fads and fashions and the preponderance of management gurus who prescribe courses of action without any substantive basis in evidence. Good empirical studies are rare.

Clarifying the nature of change is also desirable. Sometimes it is deliberate, a product of conscious reasoning and actions. This type of change may be termed *planned change*. In contrast, change can occur in a seemingly spontaneous and unplanned way – a type of change known as *emergent change*.

The importance of these two interpretations of change is that change is rarely fixed or linear but contains an important emergent element. The theory of complex adaptive systems accepts that while organizational change can be planned to a degree it can never be fully isolated from the effects of serendipity, uncertainty, ambivalence and chance (Dawson 1996).

Change can also be episodic or continuous. Episodic change might involve the replacement of one programme or strategy with another. Continuous change, on the other hand, is ongoing, evolving, incremental and cumulative. Constant adaptation is a feature of continuous change.

Change may also be developmental, transitional and transformational. Developmental change may be planned or emergent, as noted above. Transitional change seeks to achieve a known desired state that is different from the existing one. It is episodic, planned or radical. Transitional change is the basis of much of the organizational change literature and it involves unfreezing the existing organizational equilibrium, moving to a new position or state, and then freezing in a new equilibrium position. Finally, transformational change is radical in nature and requires a shift, or step change, in the assumptions made by the organization and its members. Transformation can result in an organization that differs significantly in terms of structure, processes, culture and strategy.

The impression often given is that organizational change is, or can be, a rational, controlled and orderly process. In practice, however, change can be chaotic and unpredictable, often involving shifting goals, discontinuous activities and the unexpected. Change is therefore perhaps best seen in context and therefore best understood in relation to the complex dynamic systems within which it occurs. Whole systems thinking endeavours to embrace the complexity of change in complex organizations like health services. Public health is a particularly good example of a complex activity since it spans so many organizational settings, all of which have an impact on health even if this is not necessarily their core purpose or reason for being.

Organizational development

Considerable mystique surrounds organizational development (OD), which is unhelpful and disabling. The term is interpreted in different ways by different practitioners, some seeing it as a comprehensive organization-wide development programme with particular underpinning principles and common approaches, while others use it more loosely to describe any development programme within an organization that is designed to meet organizational objectives as well as personal ones.

Although OD encompasses a huge area of management theory and practice it is not as complicated as it can seem and is largely basic common sense, though no less important for that. OD is a field of applied behavioural science that seeks to develop the principles and practice of managing change and improving effectiveness in organizations. It has been defined as

> a set of behavioural science-based theories, values, strategies and techniques aimed at the planned change of organisational work setting for the purpose of enhancing individual development and improving organisational performance, through the alteration of organisational members' on-the-job behaviours.
>
> (Porras and Robertson 1992: 722)

Four dimensions of OD are particularly important for public health. They constitute a framework within which to locate the various components that need to be addressed. The dimensions are:

- *environment and context* to provide insights into, and understanding of, the policies and politics surrounding the development of public health and tackling health inequalities across the NHS, local government, the independent sector, and so on;
- *cultural change* to ensure that the underlying core beliefs and values of the organization support the open, constructive reflection required for effective public health organizations to bring about change;
- *skills development* to ensure that people have the repertoire of skills needed to undertake the work, and the capacity and capability to deploy them effectively;
- *structural development of systems and processes* necessary to coordinate and ensure that the work is executed efficiently and optimally.

Organizations often make the mistake of concentrating their energies and efforts on developing the organizational structure required – that is, putting form before function. How often, for example, does a policy-maker or politician say: 'The priority is to get the structure right'? Of course, there is no 'right' or perfect structure – simply a less imperfect one. Of equal, if not greater, importance is work and investment to establish trust, good communication and good relationships between all members of the public health team. For this to occur successfully, effective OD requires good leadership and adequate resources.

Within each of the four dimensions are a number of specific examples where OD can make a useful contribution. One of the dimensions – cultural change – is considered further below. A second dimension – skills development in the context of leadership and management – is considered further in Chapter 7.

Making sense of culture

Culture matters. Change can often by stifled by culture. Culture constitutes the informal social aspects of an organization that influences how people think, what they regard as important, and how they behave and interact at work (Mannion *et al.* 2005). Organizational culture has been defined by Schein as

> the pattern of shared basic assumptions – invented, discovered or developed by a given group as it learns to cope with its problems of external adaptation and internal integration – that has worked well enough to be considered valid and, therefore, to be taught to new members as the correct way to perceive, think, and feel in relation to those problems.
>
> (Schein 1985)

As Mannion, Davies and Marshall (with Scott) put it, culture is therefore not merely that which is observable in social life but also the shared cognitive and symbolic context within which a society or institution can be understood (Mannion *et al.* 2005). For example, a biomedical (in contrast to a social) understanding of health and illness dominates the majority of organizations concerned with the delivery of health care and therefore exerts significant influence, possibly covertly rather than overtly. Such a biomedical conception of health is deeply ingrained, not just in health care organizations but throughout society. Whenever there is any mention of health, it is the medical model that is either invoked or implied. In the context of health improvement, however, which is concerned with populations as well as individuals and with a whole systems perspective in regard to the determinants of health, a biomedical perspective is inappropriate. Such a bias is in keeping with the dominance of a medical culture that pervades not only health care organizations but often public conceptions more generally of what constitutes health. There are many successful examples of where organizations have demonstrated a corporate social responsibility for health by seeking to improve the environment in which individuals make their healthy choices. But they still tend to be the exception.

If organizations are to take health improvement seriously then they need to change their culture and mindset accordingly, using OD and CM tools to assist in bringing about the necessary shift. Work on cultural change suggests that while it is relatively easy to change certain artefacts, such as language, mission statements, and particular systems, the deeper assumptions governing behaviour may be more difficult to shift and have the potential to negate, attenuate or redirect the change effort (Harris and Ogbonna 2002). Indeed, such difficulties seem to underlie the conclusion in the Wanless report on public health that despite 'numerous policy initiatives being directed towards public health they have not succeeded in rebalancing health policy away from the short-term imperatives of health care' (Wanless 2004: 6).

While there is much talk of culture change there is little practice guidance available on how to deliver it on the ground. Most recently in the context of public health and health improvement, the UK government has been attracted to what social marketing can offer by way of reinforcing positive messages about health aimed not just at individuals and behavioural change at this level but also at organizations and social mores more generally (National Social Marketing Centre 2006). Social marketing has been defined by the National Social Marketing Centre as 'the systematic application of marketing concepts and techniques to achieve specific behavioural goals, for a social or public good', and health-related social marketing has been defined as 'the systematic application of marketing concepts and techniques, to achieve specific behavioural goals to improve health and reduce health inequalities'.

Social marketing is not designed or intended to replace other aspects of public health. It is part of the toolkit that can be used in a strategic way, to inform the mix of interventions such as regulatory action, or practical, hands-on methods to support specific behaviour change. As the report from the National Social Marketing Centre makes clear, 'actions that focus on individuals and wider society factors need to go together' (2006: 4).

CONCLUSION

The rise of management in health systems is a global phenomenon and has been much in evidence over the past thirty years or so. Central to all managerial reforms has been a technocratic faith in improved management and in its capacity to resolve deep-seated, and essentially political, problems. The arrival of New Public Management in the 1990s heralded the attempt once again to inject scientific rigour and rational problem-solving. Though somewhat discredited in sectors like health, it remains a potent force and holds wide appeal to reforming policy-makers. It represents a reaction to the perceived failings of what might be termed 'old' public management and a loss of faith in the ability of governments in particular to bring about effective change. But NPM suffers from its own flaws, and these are particularly evident in much public health. A new managerial paradigm is required for managing for health, drawing on notions of complex adaptive systems. This is the essence of public health management.

DISCUSSION QUESTIONS

1   Would you consider that the notion of a complex adaptive system more usefully fits the real world of public health than traditional models based on scientific management principles or New Public Management thinking?
2   How would you begin to use complexity thinking in your management role?
3   Why do you think there is a reluctance to embrace complexity thinking despite its intrinsic appeal in capturing how things are and how they work?

4   Is there a problem because many existing managers and leaders are wedded to a different, and perhaps outmoded, managerial paradigm? If so, what actions would you consider taking to confront the problem?

5   Does the notion of public health management help you make sense of the management challenge in public health and the skills required to meet it?

REFERENCES

Aldersalde, R. and Hunter, D.J. (1994) Commissioning and public health. *Journal of Management and Medicine*, 8(6): 20–31.

Blackler, F. (2006) Chief executives and the modernisation of the English National Health Service, *Leadership*, 2(1): 5–30.

Calman, K. (1998) *The potential for health: how to improve the nation's health*. Oxford: Oxford University Press.

Chapman, J. (2004) *System failure: why governments must learn to think differently*, 2nd edition. London: Demos.

Choi, B.C.K., Hunter, D.J., Tsou, W. and Sainsbury, P. (2005) Diseases of comfort: primary cause of death in the 22nd century. *Journal of Epidemiology & Community Health*, 59(12): 1030–1034.

Dawson, S.J.N.D. (1996) *Analysing organisations*. Basingstoke: Macmillan.

Degeling, P.J., Maxwell, S.A., Iedema, R. and Hunter, D.J. (2004) Making clinical governance work. *British Medical Journal*, 329: 679–681.

Department of Health (1998) *The health of the nation – a policy assessed*. London: HMSO.

Department of Health (2001) *The report of the chief medical officer's project to strengthen the public health function*. London: Department of Health.

Glouberman, S. (2000) *Towards a new perspective on health and health policy: a synthesis document of the health network*. Ottawa: Canadian Policy Research Networks.

Goodwin, N. (2006) *Leadership in health care: a European perspective*. London: Routledge.

Griffiths, R. (1983) *NHS management inquiry report*. London: DHSS.

Hafferty, F.W. and McKinlay, J.B. (eds) (1993) *The changing medical profession: an international perspective*. New York: Oxford University Press.

Handy, C. (1994) *The empty raincoat: making sense of the future*. London: Hutchinson.

Harris, L.C. and Ogbonna, E. (2002) The unintended consequences of culture interventions: a study of unexpected outcomes. *British Journal of Management*, 13: 31–49.

Hood, C. (1991) A public management for all seasons? *Public Administration*, 69(1): 3–19.

Hunter, D.J. (1999) *Managing for health: implementing the new health agenda.* London: Institute for Public Policy Research.

Hunter, D.J. (2002) *Public health management: making it a world concern.* Report of WHO/University of Durham Meeting. Geneva: WHO.

Hunter, D.J. (2006) From tribalism to corporatism: the continuing managerial challenge to medical dominance, in D. Kelleher, J. Gabe and G. Williams (eds) *Challenging medicine,* 2nd edition. London: Routledge, pp. 1–23.

Hunter, D.J. and Berman, P.C. (1997) Public health management: time for a new start? *European Journal of Public Health,* 7(3): 345–349.

Hunter, D.J. and Marks, L. (2005) *Managing for health: what incentives exist for NHS managers to focus on wider healthy issues?* London: King's Fund.

Iles, V. and Sutherland, K. (2001) *Organisational change. a review for health care managers, professionals and researchers.* London: National Co-ordinating Committee Service Delivery and Organisation.

Institute of Medicine (2003) *The future of the public's health in the 21st century.* Washington: National Academies Press.

Jewell, T. (1999) Public health practice in health authorities, in S. Griffiths and D.J. Hunter (eds) *Perspectives in public health.* Oxford: Radcliffe Medical Press, pp. 159–170.

Kotter, J. (1982) *The general manager.* New York: Free Press.

Legowski, B. and McKay, L. (2000) *Health beyond health care: twenty-five years of federal health policy development.* CPRN Discussion Paper No. H/04. Ottawa: Canadian Policy Research Networks.

McPherson, K. (2001) Are disease prevention initiatives working? *The Lancet,* 357: 1790–1792.

Mannion, R., Davies, H.U.W. and Marshall, M.N. (2005) *Cultures for performance in health care.* Maidenhead: Open University Press.

Marquhand, D. (2005) Monarchy, state and dystopia. *The Political Quarterly,* 76(3): 333–336.

Milburn, A. (2000) *A healthier nation and a healthier economy: the contribution of a modern NHS.* LSE Health Annual Lecture, 8 March. London: London School of Economics.

Mintzberg, H. (1980) Structure in 5s: a synthesis of the research on organisation design. *Management in Science,* 226: 332.

Moore, M. (1996) *Public sector reform: downsizing, restructuring, improving perform-ance.* Discussion Paper No. 7. Geneva: World Health Organization.

Morone, J.A. (1993) The health care bureaucracy: small changes, big consequences. *Journal of Health Politics, Policy and Law,* 18: 723–739.

National Social Marketing Centre (2006) *It's our health! Realising the potential of effective social marketing.* London: National Consumer Council.

Nutbeam, D. and Wise, M. (2002) Structures and strategies for public health intervention, in R. Detels, J. McEwen, R. Beaglehole and H. Tanaka (eds) *Oxford textbook of public health,* Volume 3: *The practice of public health,* 4th edition, Oxford: Oxford University Press, pp. 1873–1888.

Osborne, D. and Gaebler, T. (1993) *Reinventing government: how the entrepreneurial spirit is transforming the public sector.* New York: Plume.

Plsek, P. (2006) An organisation is not a machine! Principles for managing complex adaptive systems. Materials prepared for Leadership for Health Improvement Programme. York.

Plsek, P.E. and Greenhalgh, T. (2001) The challenge of complexity in health care. *British Medical Journal,* 323: 625–628.

Porras, J. and Robertson, P. (1992) Organisation development, in M. Dunnette and L. Hough (eds) *Handbook of industrial and organisational psychology,* 3. Palo Alto: Consulting Psychologists Press, pp. 719–822.

Schein, E. (1985) *Organisational culture and leadership.* San Francisco: Jossey-Bass.

Schon, D. (1973) *Beyond the stable state.* Harmondsworth: Penguin.

Secretary of State for Health (2006) *Our health, our care, our say: a new direction for community services.* Cm 6737. London: HMSO.

Stewart, J. (1998) Advance or retreat: from the traditions of public administration to the New Public Management and beyond, *Public Policy and Administration,* 13(4): 12–27.

Taylor, F.W. (1911) *Principles of scientific management.* New York: Harper.

Wanless, D. (2002) *Securing our future health: taking a long-term view.* Final report. London: HM Treasury.

Wanless, D. (2004) *Securing good health for the whole population.* Final report. London: HM Treasury.

World Bank (1993) *World development report: investing in health.* New York: Oxford University Press.

Wylie, I., Griffiths, S. and Hunter, D.J. (1999) Everywhere and nowhere – a Socratic dialogue on the new public health. *British Medical Journal,* 319: 839–840.

Chapter 4

Managers for health
Skills and knowledge frameworks

Mats Brommels and Alison McCallum

KEY POINTS OF THIS CHAPTER

- Globalization is reshaping communities both in the developed and developing parts of the world
- Communities are increasingly multiethnic and multicultural with growing socio-economic divisions aggravated by a rising consumerism among the resourceful
- Poverty and life style related ill-health continue to be a challenge; in addition, societally related health threats like deprivation and violence will increase
- Traditional public health management is successful where it can rely on medical research and professional intrasectoral and intersectoral actions
- The increasingly complex environments and health challenges require a broader approach and new skills from public health managers
- Those new skills include stakeholder, network, change and complexity informed management

INTRODUCTION

The chapter opens with a case study of a small community in transition in order to show the range and complexity of public health problems with which public health practitioners have to deal.

CASE STUDY

Westlinns: a community in transition

Westlinns is a community of approximately 125,000 inhabitants. The centre of population, Linnburgh (population 100,000), comprises a picturesque village that dates back several hundred years and is surrounded by a new town development that grew from the post Second World War manufacturing boom. The vision of a city in the country where workers' families could grow up healthy was quickly overtaken by the rapidly constructed, minimum-standard, high-density social housing found in many European countries that is characterized by damp, mould, cold homes and, at best, loss of optimism among the residents. The loss of the mines and heavy manufacturing has improved air quality, but the populations who worked at, and live close to, the old sites, and who are among the least affluent, will have been at greater risk of exposure to environmental hazards.

Traditionally, Linnburgh was a resting place for travellers to the cities at opposite sides of the country, particularly those who arrived by boat. Westlinns is still home to a gypsy traveller population but, while there have always been small numbers of immigrants, people from minority ethnic groups now comprise 15 per cent of the population. There are five main groups. First, small long-established communities, like the gypsy travellers and those who came as refugees before and during the Second World War; not all of this group can be identified from the statistics. Next, second and third generations of immigrant families from India, Pakistan, Bangladesh and East Africa; third, highly skilled individuals from elsewhere in the country, Europe, the Indian subcontinent and South-East Asia attracted by the job opportunities; fourth, refugees and asylum seekers, mostly from the Balkans and Africa; and, fifth, those from less prosperous parts of the former Soviet Union and China who enter the country illegally and work in insecure and unsafe conditions.

To the north, Linnburgh village becomes rich farmland that runs down to the river. At this point the river is used mostly for recreation, but to the east the river is wider. Here, there is a large gas terminal and a port, principally used for freight. On the other side of the motorway that runs through Westlinns to join two university cities are five ex-mining areas, a mixture of villages and small clusters of houses. Although 85–90 per cent of the population live within a five-minute drive of their general practitioner and 30 minutes drive from the hospital and out-of-hours service, between 30 and 40 per cent of the population of these villages don't have access to a car.

During the recession 20 years ago the mines closed and only minor parts of the old manufacturing industries survived. As those workplaces disappeared, so did the sources of stable jobs for skilled and unskilled workers of all ages. In around 30 per cent of families, in three of the ex-mining villages and two of the neighbourhoods in Linnburgh, there are men aged 35 who have never worked and men who have not worked steadily for 20 years. Around 20 per cent of the women

81

in these communities found part-time jobs making computer components, though these disappeared at the end of the technology boom six years ago. The skilled and unskilled manual work has been replaced by largely part-time posts in service industries; many of the current vacancies, even for skilled workers, boast that they exceed the national minimum wage. Most unskilled women, for example, are now employed by the public sector, as shift workers in the large supermarket, or the retail park at the side of the motorway. In one ex-mining village, however, although the unemployment rate is now low, 3.9 per cent, many more, 38 per cent, are economically inactive, 13 per cent are unable to work because of illness or disability, 10 per cent are unpaid carers and 48 per cent of adults have no educational qualifications. Here, around 25 per cent of the children live in workless households.

In Linnburgh old village, the indicators of health and well-being are almost a mirror image of those in the ex-industrial areas. Female life expectancy is just less than 87 years, compared with less than 74 years in the mining villages, only 5 per cent of the children live in workless households, only 7 per cent of the women smoke during pregnancy compared with around 50 per cent. Families that moved to the new town areas that developed in the 1950s and 1960s are growing old together, just as their houses and traditional forms of service provision are showing signs of age and loss of function.

One of the mining villages has become a mini-centre for small-scale high technology business, but the populations of the others are dwindling. At the same time, young families are moving into new estates on green and brownfield sites on the outskirts of Linnburgh, attracted by the motorway and rail links to the university cities, and the affordable house prices. The availability of social housing was also one of the reasons that the national government gave for having allocated places for 300 refugee and asylum-seeker families to Westlinns over the last five years. The geographical concentration of social housing has meant that each school has taken around ten children per year with additional language needs. Functional illiteracy is a more widespread problem, however, affecting around 15 per cent of the population – males more than females.

The industrial and rural past of the area lives on with a steady stream of cases of communicable disease, including sexually transmitted diseases, tuberculosis, newer infections like E.Coli 0157, and regular, though diminishing numbers of outbreaks of salmonella and cryptosporidiosis. While numbers of cases are small in a population of this size, the potential for large-scale outbreaks associated with large functions, a failure of farming, food processing, or the drinking-water infrastructure remains. Teenagers are taking advantage of the drop-in clinic after school at the advice centre and internet café. Here, 10 per cent of those who have taken chlamydia testing kits have tested positive. Teenage pregnancies are a problem in certain parts of Westlinns, with crude rates ranging from 2–28 per 100 women aged 13–19 years, in line with deprivation.

Use of legal and illegal substances remains a problem with age-standardized admission rates for alcohol-related problems of just under 1,000 per 100,000 population. These rates are fairly consistent across communities, with significantly lower rates found only in the most affluent areas and the communities with the largest concentration of minority ethnic groups.

Violence has lately become an increasing source of concern, with two distinct types of epidemiology. Assault-related injuries peak during weekends along the 'pub and bar trails' at the outskirts of Linnburgh, calling for joint efforts of the health and social services and the local police. Domestic violence is on the rise in deprived areas, mainly resulting in traumas and injuries of variable severity. Homicides are a feature of organized crime, but may also hit young women. Although those instances are rare, they are a tragic consequence of the paternalistic cultures of some minority groups.

Socio-economic differences in health, education, lifestyle and opportunity have grown as more affluent populations in Westlinns have been quicker to stop smoking, change their diet, take advantage of private leisure facilities, the cycle and walking routes along the environmentally improved old railway and canal-side. The market does not provide for groups at risk. Attempts by the health and local authorities to ring-fence funding for health promotion have made those activities vulnerable to cost-cutting, short-term funding of isolated projects and limited engagement of the public in assessing their needs and developing effective and acceptable projects to meet them.

The health service, however, is not the only source of effort and expertise to improve the health of the public. The local authority for the area, Westlinns Council, provides a mixture of legally required and discretionary services including economic development, trading standards, transport, roads, property and housing, planning, arts and leisure, education, environmental health, social care and practical support. The religious communities organize several of the ethnic groups and also provide a number of social and support services. A number of voluntary organizations are active in Westlinns; they cover a wide range of activities, including leisure activities, activities for children and adolescents, retired and elderly people, as well as sports and cultural activities.

TRADITIONAL PUBLIC HEALTH ACTIONS

A snapshot of public health management

The method of assessing the health of communities by comparing birth and death — how and when it occurs, and the size and the nature of the differences between populations — has long historical traditions. In many countries the Church collected these detailed records originally; they enabled statistics to be collected for each parish. Analysis of the records illuminated the differences in life expectancy experienced by people with modest or affluent backgrounds and between different communities. Among the earliest community profiles were the parish descriptions that resulted from the responses to standard questions provided by the local ministers. These were designed as 'An inquiry into the state of the country for the purpose of ascertaining the quantum of happiness enjoyed by its inhabitants, and the means of its future improvement'.

Presently, surveillance of the health of the population utilizes a wide range of data, covering health risks, morbidity, mortality and the utilization of health services and health and social benefits. The possibility to increase the scope, specificity and coverage of health-related data is greatly enhanced by administrative and clinical information being processed by electronic systems and thus made easily retrievable. Increasingly, countries establish disease- or patient-group specific registers, to which health care providers also submit data on clinical outcome as well as indicators of clinical and service quality. Many clinical programmes record patient-reported, health-related quality of life on a routine basis, thus, as in old times, attempting to measure 'the quantum of happiness'.

Public health managers use the epidemiological and service utilization data of their populations to identify risks of both acute and chronic illness as well as the need for interventions by health professionals, measures to be taken by public authorities, activities to be promoted in the communities, and information and education needs among the population. Those assessments are combined into community diagnoses reflecting risks related to all determinants for health.

Preventive services were originally focused on communicable diseases control and maternity and child care. Increasingly, activities also cover the control of risks of chronic diseases, and focus on ill-health both in individuals and in the community. Reflecting the manifold determinants of health they pay attention to personal lifestyles and the need for consorted actions by a number of societal stakeholders. Increasingly, preventive services take the form of health promotion campaigns.

Environmental health – the control of the health risks of everyday life, including housing conditions and workplaces, and traditionally focusing on activities like inspections of food-processing and sanitary conditions – is in many countries part of public health services.

Strengths and weaknesses

Traditional preventive services have by and large been successful. The development of antenatal care – weighing and measuring children, nutritional support for mother and child, etc. – has drastically reduced infant mortality. The control of communicable diseases relies on case reporting from health care providers and central processing and analysis of data, which enables the identification of peaks in incidence and clusters of cases. Some intersectoral actions have had very favourable outcomes. Road safety has improved by investments in roads and infrastructure, legislation and public information campaigns. Considerable efforts have been made to reduce environmental health hazards. Accident prevention, both in general and in population groups like children, workers and the elderly, has resulted in considerable reductions in the numbers of accidents and the incidence of accident-related injuries.

Public health actions require the local population at risk to buy into the proposed programme and the rationale behind it. This is highlighted by a comparison between the UK and Finland. Because of the distrust of science (attributed to BSE and similar failures of government response in Britain) and the lack of knowledge, outbreaks of measles and mumps occurred following the declining uptake of the mumps, measles and rubella (MMR) vaccine. In Finland the MMR campaign engaged all child health centres, parents were informed by a nationwide catch-up campaign, and the military inoculated all its recruits. Those measures, in combination with national reporting and serological confirmation, led to 40 per cent of the population being immunized with 95 per cent coverage of the population at risk.

Effective public health management requires data to be collected on the population, its health and health service use. As health services change, particularly as the result of increasing decentralization, the data reporting 'infrastructure' and 'culture' may become fragmented and difficult to coordinate. The challenge is of growing importance as the population ages, making seamless care across organizational boundaries crucial. If those 'chains of care' are not reflected in the information stream, important data on the need for the continuity of care and access to services might be lost.

The challenges of current public health management are reflected in data, indicating both successes and failures. Population figures show an absolute reduction in ill health, but increasing negative effects of socio-economic differences at the same time. Health care services and professionals have been successful in well-defined health promotion programmes like smoke cessation, whereas attempts at wider community mobilization usually have been disappointing. New communicable diseases threats, where control could rely on medical research and clinical actions (Legionella and SARS), were successfully met, whereas the more complex problem of HIV/AIDS has reached pandemic proportions in some regions of the world.

In conclusion, and echoing a theme of this book, traditional public health can be said to be strong on analysis and weak on action. One reason might be an over-reliance on a rational planning model, and under-application of theories from non-medical fields, which could be employed in the interpretation of data and give advice on suitable implementation strategies. The lack of understanding of motivational factors and drivers for change might explain the difficulties to mobilize people and communities. The length of time from the dissemination of information on health needs and risks for ill health to the adoption of corrective measures among communities at greatest risk can be seen as a failure of the advocacy role of public health. Although well aware of the need for intersectoral action, public health managers might underestimate the need for direct political involvement and influence. This is also reflected in frequent failures to mobilize secure funding streams for public health.

NEW TRENDS AND FRAMEWORKS

The reality facing the public health manager

The case of Westlinns, with which the chapter opened, reminds us of the reality that is facing public health managers today. The buzz word is 'complexity'. The main sources of complexity are the increasing globalization, the changing disease panorama, and the rise of consumer activism in health and social care.

The effects of the globalized economy with reduced barriers to the flow of information, capital, goods and services, and labour, are dramatic both in the developed and developing parts of the world. The transfer of labour-intensive industries to low-income countries has changed the local economies and labour markets in Western countries, with increasing unemployment and a need for both manual and white-collar workers to retrain and find new job opportunities. At the same time migration brings millions of people from developing to developed countries. The receiving countries have to adjust to changing multiethnic and multicultural societies, and to integrate immigrants into their new communities. In many countries the process is far from successful, leading to the establishment of closed immigrant communities with high unemployment and crime rates. In several receiving countries self-employment is the only realistic alternative for immigrants, and many service industries are highly dominated by immigrants. In Western European countries the traditional liberal values and tolerant attitudes to foreign cultures have eroded. Extremist groups have emerged and social tensions have lately erupted in unrest and even large-scale violence.

Previous optimistic views on the continuous reduction of health problems, as improved living conditions reduced poverty-related diseases like infectious diseases, have had to be revised. Lifestyle related chronic diseases did not 'replace' the poverty-related ones, but were 'superimposed' upon them, especially when assessed on a global scale. In addition, infectious diseases change their manifestations and are an increasing threat in the developed world also. Society-related diseases like domestic and street violence, as well as terrorism, are recent additions to the disease panorama. Public health has to fight against all three categories.

Patients, relatives and citizens at large are increasingly turning into well-informed and demanding consumers. Medical knowledge and information on health services and their performance are increasingly accessible over the internet. Consumer groups organize in health and social care, and play an increasingly important role in decision-making at the national, regional and local levels.

Rising health care consumerism is beginning to be reflected in national legislation. The Finnish case is especially interesting. Traditionally, health care legislation defined the provision of health services for the population as a responsibility of public authorities. A recent constitutional reform defines access to health and social care according to need as a basic human right. Accordingly, administrative courts have, based on patient complaints, begun to issue verdicts forcing authorities to provide services to the complainant.

Given this complexity, the prevailing management model in public health, based on community diagnoses, expert assessment of the need for public health interventions and the social planning model (Rosenau 1994) guiding intersectoral actions and community development, is too limited. There is an even greater need than previously for a holistic approach to public health management of the type articulated in Chapter 3.

Alternative frameworks

Consumerism and empowerment

We define the 'consumer behaviour' of patients and relatives as the actions of highly informed individuals who want to have a greater say in decisions concerning their health, disease and care. Consumers are organized into interest groups that are vocal, seek benefits for their members, exercise pressure on decision-makers, and provide services, including professional services, to members.

Health promotion is the part of the larger health system, which has most consistently employed a customer approach. Health promotion, according to the Ottawa Charter (WHO 1986), has the goal of enabling people to gain control over their health determinants and thus their health, and to take responsibility for improving their health. People are seen as active participating subjects, not the passive objects of professional evaluation and intervention. An often-used synonym to 'enabling' is empowerment.

Koelen and Lindström (2005), in their article on health promotion, make a distinction between community empowerment, referring to a group of people, and individual empowerment, which they specifically address. They identify four factors influencing individual empowerment:

- health locus of control;
- learned helplessness;
- perceived self-efficacy;
- outcomes expectation.

The first two relate to the personal experience of controllability, failure or success. A belief in the locus of control being external is difficult to change, but learned

87

helplessness can be overcome by creating experiences of success. That leads to perceived self-efficacy. A positive assessment of the probability that a specific action will lead to an aimed outcome increases the individual's willingness to undertake that action. That assessment can be influenced by information and advice, whereas perceived lack of control is a greater challenge. Positive experience has been gained from step-by-step reattribution interventions aimed at helping people to gain confidence. The authors point out that an empowerment process is enhanced by a partnership rather than a hierarchical relation between professionals and clients.

Conditions for creating a partnership are further analysed by Anderson and Funnell (2005) in relation to diabetes care. They see the change as a paradigm shift (from the acute care model), which potentially will take a long time and requires professionals to truly realize the value of patients' self-management in terms of health outcomes. The shift is enhanced by professionals exercising reflective practice and professional leaders becoming advocates for patient-centred collaboration. The role of educator and advocate would fit well with that of public health manager.

Community empowerment is a 'social action process that promotes the participation of people, organizations and communities towards the goals of increased individual and community control, political efficacy, improved quality of community life, and social justice' (Wallerstein 1992). One way for public health authorities, managers and practitioners to contribute to community empowerment could be to establish contacts with community groups and – as in the case of the individual – by information and training enable the community to increase its control. An alternative approach would be to acknowledge that empowerment on a community level will more readily take place when initiated from within by a social movement.

A social movement is a group action organized by mostly informal networks of individuals with a specific cause. Tarrow (1994) defines a social movement as collective challenges undertaken by people with common purposes and solidarity in sustained interactions with elites, opponents and authorities. Social movements can take different forms and strategies. Campaigns are organized and sustained effort are sought by making claims on a target authority. Political actions are the formation of special purpose groups, building coalitions with other groups with similar agendas, public meetings and demonstrations, petitions, pamphlets and media appearances (Tilly 2004). Social movements usually have their roots in protests against social injustice, and they played an important role in the creation of democratic and equitable societies. As social movements were enhanced by the industrialization and urbanization that brought people closer to each other in the nineteenth century, one might expect that communication technology in the twenty-first century has the potential to create social movements across geographical boundaries.

Landzelius (2006) presents an example of a contemporary social movement – 'parents of preemies', a network of parents and carers of prematurely born babies hospitalized in neonatal intensive care units. She describes how the group has two agendas for parental empowerment: required access to and participation in the care of the infant, and greater representational authority over neonatal intensive care in public decision-making. The strategy with which those objectives were achieved has been to create working relationships with medical practitioners and become proficient in understanding and using the sophisticated care technology. The author points out that the success of the social movement comes with a cost: parents have been 'co-opted' and 'disciplined' into the professional arena of neonatal medicine, and are possibly dominated by the very profession they wanted to influence.

One possible approach to create interest among individuals and groups and increase their ability to take action is to use social marketing (Kotler *et al.* 2002). Social marketing applies commercial marketing methods to populations in order to motivate those to positive social change (Hastings and McDermott 2006; National Social Marketing Centre 2006). In many countries, notably the UK, it is regarded as an important tool to bring about change in individual lifestyles and is a cornerstone of government policy (Secretary of State for Health 2004). A social marketing programme consists of the following elements:

- researching the social marketing environment, including the identification of needs and resources;
- defining the target audience and the objectives and goals of the marketing effort;
- developing marketing strategies by designing the market offering;
- choosing the place and making access convenient;
- creating messages and selecting communications channels;
- managing the costs of the targeted behaviour change;
- managing the execution of the marketing plan, including budgets and funds, implementation and evaluation.

In summary, alternatives to the traditional management model governing the public health function, based on expert assessment and the social planning model, are to acknowledge that individuals and groups will be more prone to change if their motivation is intrinsic, and more successful if they are empowered to take responsibility for the actions that carry positive effects on their health. Examples from health promotion show that self-efficacy can be enhanced by information, and perceived lack of control with 'reattribution' exercises. When groups and communities realize that they can take action, they create momentum by using the collective force and strategies of a social movement. Public health managers need to see their role as partners rather than representatives of a public authority, and engage in information transfer, education and advocacy for client needs.

A critique

Some social scientists make the case that the social planning model of public health organizing does not fit well with post-modern concepts and observations of the world. Modern social planning assumes rationality, goal ordering, causality, prediction, feedback and self-correction, and attributes a special authority to the expert. Post-modernists question these assumptions and make the case that social planning eliminates diversity, and thus runs the risk of ending in disorder and deteriorated life conditions (Rosenau 1994).

Post-modernists also point out that social movements require organizational skills comparable to those found in formal organizations. Social movement leaders do mobilize community members and persuade them that they can and should take action. They increase participation in the community, but direct the attention of members to the goal of achieving specific changes in the environment. Post-modernists see those movements as hierarchical and too convinced of the justice of their goals, thus eliminating the establishment of responsibility and initiation of action among the members, and too prone on leading the troops rather than responding to their wishes (Rosenau 1994).

Post-modern planning, it is suggested, is participatory and 'involves the social collectivity in all its heterogeneous forms' (Rosenau 1994: 320). Post-modern activism stands for pluralism that contrasts with the dogmatism of modern social movements. Divergent political orientations are usual. Typical are temporary coalitions with other groups that share the same interests for the time being. As interests change, they look for new partners to team up with, and move in and out of networks. Post-modern movements are loosely knit and 'antihierarchy'. They accept members with various backgrounds, as long as they share the same 'core interest'. Members, on the other hand, look upon their engagement as temporary and part-time (Rosenau 1994).

If the post-modernist description of life is 'realistic', public health management needs to pay attention to the special characteristics of social movements cited above. The effects of targeted actions will tend to be increasingly uncertain, and the impact of expert knowledge would – on the surface – further decrease. On the other hand, the strategies described would still be workable.

LEADING PUBLIC HEALTH IN A COMPLEX WORLD

Reflecting on the alternative frameworks, four important knowledge and skills areas need to be added to the competence profile of the public health manager: managing stakeholders, managing networks, managing change, and managing complex systems.

Stakeholder management

Traditionally, public health has dealt with professional services in the health sector as well as different branches of local, regional and national government. The emergence of health promotion and community involvement as new features of public health made targeted populations and groups of citizens new stakeholders of increasing importance. Managing stakeholder relations is now a more challenging task than previously, when the task was to communicate with other professionals and to present well-argued proposals for decision-makers. These tasks remain vitally important, especially given that when it comes to presenting sound business cases for their proposals and the provision of strong advocacy for these, public health managers have often felt ill-equipped and at a disadvantage.

When addressing stakeholder groups it is helpful to identify their main drivers. Those are of three major kinds: self-interest or group interest (political decision-makers and pressure groups), client benefit (professional groups), and compassion (voluntary worker groups). The drivers – attractors to use 'complexity-speak' – need to be taken into consideration when planning relations building.

The overarching goal of an organization's stakeholder management is to raise interest among a target audience in the objectives and actions of the organization, to influence decision-making of importance to the organization, and to secure financial and other forms of support. As client groups increasingly have to be motivated and invited to take personal responsibility and action rather than to be told, informed or educated to comply with a recommended intervention, the same kind of communicating strategies that are suitable for adoption with other stakeholders should be employed in relation to client groups.

Influencing stakeholders, over which an organization does not have 'managerial control', is best done by advocacy or lobbying. The two strategies overlap, with lobbying having a slightly more negative connotation. Advocacy is defined as 'the process of convincing leaders and decision makers to use their powers and influence to support one issues or cause' (Nukuro 2000: 2). Advocacy is typically exercised by non-governmental organizations and civil society groups. They use factual presentations, persuasion and actions to promote their causes. Strategies include interpersonal communication, group communication, special events, media coverage and high-level meetings. The target audience includes opinion-leaders, decision-makers and journalists. The Johns Hopkins University Center for Communication Program identifies six steps in a successful advocacy campaign: analysis, strategy, mobilization, action, evaluation and community. Increasingly, advocacy is used as a strategy for reaching target audiences for health promotion programmes (Nukuro 2000).

Lobbying is 'an attempt by an individual or an organisation to influence public policy decisions' (Brown and Evens 2000: 321). Lobbying is typically used by interest groups rather than formal organizations. Interest groups that have a common ideology and members with a high degree of devotion are usually the most effective ones. Large interest groups have difficulties to create the same internal cohesion, but might be influential because of the number of their members.

Lobbying is divided into two categories: direct and indirect. Direct lobbying aims at policy-makers, indirect lobbying tries to influence public opinion more generally.

In direct lobbying the opinions and preferences of an interest group are communicated to decision-makers, quite often by a professional representative of the group (lobbyist). Lobbying is increasingly a full-time profession, which attracts lawyers, former politicians and bureaucrats. Services offered include legal advice, public relations, advertising, coalition-building, fund-raising, polling and event planning (Brown and Evens 2000).

Indirect or grassroots lobbying focuses on targeting individuals outside the policy-making arena. Activities are typically mailing campaigns, advertising, writing letters to the editor, as well as public meetings and demonstrations (Brown and Evens 2000).

Lobbying messages should, according to standard advertising practices, do the following: command attention, cater to the heart and head, clarify the message, communicate a benefit, create trust, call for action, and be consistent (Nukuro 2000).

One way of increasing the effectiveness of advocacy and lobbying is to team up with other interest groups in advocacy networks. In forming a network it is important to establish a clear purpose and shared mission and to build commitment by participatory processes. In the maintenance and growth phase an organizational structure is needed, although it should be loose. Skills needs should be analysed, and, based on the analysis, a recruitment policy should be decided upon. An internal communication system is a necessity. Leadership is shared by using coordinating committees and rotation of tasks. Meetings should be organized only when needed, and properly managed (Nukuro 2000).

Network management

In addition to the advocacy networks mentioned, public health managers will increasingly rely on networks of organizations that provide services and professional advice related to public health. Public authorities are looking for possibilities to contract-out services they once provided themselves, and public health departments will be no exception. Consequently, public health departments will not only act as contractors but will also seek cooperation with organizations that independently provide services in the public health field.

Public health managers will have to master two forms of network management: vertical and horizontal. Vertically, the manager is the principal to a number of agents, bound by contracts specifying deliverables, incentives and possible sanctions. Horizontally, the manager coordinates organizations that are involved in a joint production process, a 'service implementation network' (Milward and Provan 2003).

Trust and the right incentives will facilitate work across organizational boundaries. Milward and Provan (2003) suggest that coordination is best provided by a 'supra organisation', which they call a 'network administrative organisation (NAO)'. The public health department would fit well into that role, especially as it also funds some of the involved collaborating organizations. To be an effective NAO it should occupy a wide enough segment of the service chain in order to protect the value of its own contribution (Miles and Snow 1992). That echoes in an interesting way the recent literature on governance, recommending 'indirect governance' by a professionally competent third-party acting on behalf of the principal (Salamon 2002; Tuohy 2003).

Coordination of the service implementation network involves organizing cooperation, contracting, planning and monitoring contracts and agreements. The focus should be on programmes rather than organizations (Milward and Provan 2003). Stability promotes network performance, but networks are inherently unstable. The network manager is, therefore, involved in negotiations and contract monitoring with 'wheeling and dealing' counterparts. Tasks can be contracted out, but legitimacy is difficult to transfer.

No evidence suggests that there is one best practice or a specific organizational form that has positive effects on networks. The network manager has to rely on 'muddling through' and adapt to the particular circumstances in a given context. Cooperation is enhanced by social control such as occupational socialization, collective sanctions and reputation ('agency push theory'). Organizations form collaborative links as the funder decides on requirements or recommendations ('institutional pull theory') (Milward and Provan 2003). The skilful network manager acts by utilizing this knowledge on network behaviour.

Change management

Theories of change focus both on individual and organizational change. The self-change model of Prochaska *et al.* (1994) is widely applied in health promotion. The authors identify a 'chain of change', including a long preparatory phase, marked by making the need for change conscious, creating engagement by emotional arousal, securing commitment by continuing self-re-evaluation, and maintaining sustainability by suitable environmental control, rewards and helping relationships. These phases apply also to groups of individuals and organizations.

Changes in organizations and work processes from the 1950s onwards were often organized as organizational development (OD). A text-book definition of OD is:

> A top-management supported, long range effort to improve an organiza-
> tion's problem-solving and renewal processes, particularly through a more
> effective and collaborative diagnosis and management of organizational
> culture – with a special emphasis on formal work team . . . and with the
> assistance of a consultant facilitator . . .
>
> (French and Bell 1990: 17)

The roots of OD lie in Kurt Lewin's 'action research', a systematic approach to change organized as a cycle of diagnosis, planning, action, evaluation and feedback. Action research is an appealing approach in a public health programme that aims to engage a target group, stimulate its members to take responsibility for their own actions, and create local ownership. In addition to facilitator skills the support person also needs to have the capacity to organize a continuous, process-oriented study of the change itself.

Later, the term 'learning organization' was coined by P.M. Senge. A learning organization promotes and rewards personal mastery, uncovers mental models ('deeply engrained assumptions which affect the way individuals think about people, situations and organizations' [Senge 1990: 8]), fosters a shared vision among organization members, and emphasizes team learning and systems thinking. A learning organization, according to Garvin (1993), encourages systemic problem-solving, active experimentation, an inquiry into the experience and history of the organization, utilizes the experience of others, and promotes effective internal communication.

A growing body of knowledge gained from continuous medical education and clinical guidelines implementation indicates what works in changing professional practice. A learning approach is potentially more successful than change initiatives based on managerial directives or campaigns. Effective learning is self-directed, problem- or action-oriented, and focuses on self-experienced challenges from practice. Under those conditions professionals are ready to receive expert feedback and advice (see, for example, Grol and Grimshaw 2003). Based on an observational study of primary care, Greer (1988) found that local practice was affected when local innovators were supported by 'idea champions' who were able to communicate in a colloquial way and were supported by opinion leaders.

Especially when public health managers are reaching out to community and special interest groups aiming to empower them and create a partnership, action research strategies should be applied. That partnership could be viewed as a learning organization, applying problem- or action-oriented change strategies.

Complexity informed management

Writers on health care management have in recent years made repeated reference to the increasing complexity of health sector organizations (e.g. Anderson and McDaniel 2000; Plsek and Greenhalgh 2001). They are described as 'complex adaptive systems' and complexity and chaos theory are used in order to shed light on their behaviour.

Plsek and Greenhalgh (2001) define complex adaptive systems as follows: 'A collection of individual agents with freedom to act in ways that are not always totally predictable, and whose actions are interconnected so that one agent's actions change the context for other agents.' They list a number of organizational properties, including

- fuzzy boundaries;
- agents act on internalized rules;

94

■ agents and the system are adaptive;
■ systems overlap and co-evolve;
■ tension and paradox;
■ inherent non-linearity;
■ inherent unpredictability;
■ inherent pattern;
■ attractor behaviour;
■ self-organization through simple locally applied rules.

Chaos theory relates the following properties to non-linear systems:

■ the system is sensitive to its initial conditions;
■ dampening feedback leads to stable states, whereas amplifying feedback unstabilizes the system to the brink of disintegration;
■ the system trajectory is genuinely unpredictable, but still bounded by attractors;
■ a strange attractor creates an infinite, yet bounded system;
■ non-linear systems are adaptive and robust at the same time (Sharp and Priesmeyer 1995).

The field of public health embraces a range of stakeholders – policy-makers, regulatory agencies, professional experts and service providers, and an increasing number of community and interest groups with varying agendas and inherently unpredictable behaviour (the latter if one accepts a post-modernist view). It is not unreasonable to see it as a truly complex adaptive system.

Anderson and McDaniel (2000) draw on complexity theory in their observations on what they term 'complexity informed management'. For those with the ambition to influence the intricate network of official, public, professional, informal and lay groups and communities, it will be important to identify and honour the connections and patterns of relationships among agents, and to understand the inevitable tensions and conflicts. Rather than exercising traditional management practices, complexity informed leaders allow self-organization, understanding that status hierarchies as well as collaborative relationships will emerge. Learning occurs from daily patterns of interaction as processes and structures develop. As the system trajectory over time is fundamentally unknowable it is necessary to settle for an understanding of system boundaries and set out to develop an adaptive, yet robust system. Special attention should be paid to strange attractors.

Adaption and flexibility are enhanced by diverse, emergent and complicated strategies – there is a need to juggle many options. With fuzzy borders and an unpredictable future, sense-making and creating coherent narratives become increasingly important management tasks. Meaning is created by shared values and deep beliefs. Professions combine values, roles, rules and procedures into a whole that allows people to reflect and develop meaning. The same process can be expected to take place in an interest group with highly devoted members. Adaption is also promoted by a capacity to improvise. For improvisation expertise is essential, as well as skills developed 'at bricolage' (demonstrated as the ability to create what is needed out of whatever material is at hand).

CONCLUSION

The landscape of public health is changing as national and local economies are reshaped by globalization. Labour-intensive industries move to low-income countries and are replaced either by activities with high technology and knowledge content as well as private and public services. Large-scale immigration will change high-income countries to multiethnic and multicultural societies. Complexity and fragmentation are the main consequences of these developments.

Ill health and health risks will also show an increasing complexity. No country will be totally protected from poverty-related diseases, and the prevalence of lifestyle-related chronic disorders will increase, especially in developing regions. Societal problems will also grow in scale and intensity, given expression through rising levels of social deprivation and violence. The divisions in society will be further aggravated by rising consumerism, with well-educated and resourceful individuals demanding and getting a larger share of services, in contrast to deprived groups who will experience decreasing access to services.

Traditional approaches to the management of public health, employing professional needs assessment and expert-directed interventions, will continue to be important. But in addition, public health managers in the future will have to learn new skills in order to be able to handle the complex challenges of the global economy and post-modern values. Intersectoral actions between public agencies will remain as crucial as ever, but will have to be extended to include non-governmental organizations and community groups. The latter will in many cases be post-modern, and change shape, interest and participants over time.

The skills profile of the future public health manager will include managing stakeholders, networks and change. All three forms have a substantial body of knowledge to draw from. Stakeholder management covers the skills of mobilizing social movements and affecting public opinion, in addition to understanding and influencing power relations. Public health departments will work – in addition to offering their own professional input – through public, private and voluntary partners, but the responsibility of guaranteeing a comprehensive service will lie with the departments. They will coordinate the contributions from a plurality of agents and organizations. A specific challenge will be to enhance continuous change and development by creating communities of learning. An appropriate term to describe this wide set of skills is 'complexity informed management', focusing on shared objectives and values, and allowing self-organization to occur.

DISCUSSION QUESTIONS

1   The chapter argues that globalization is reshaping our societies into complex multiethnic and multicultural communities. Is this a correct 'community diagnosis'?

2   Public health has to manage both traditional sources of ill-health and new scourges like domestic violence, environmental hazards and terrorism. Is the task facing the public health manager a mission impossible?

3   Given the limitations of traditional public health management, do a post-modern view and complexity theory provide useful insights for managers taking on the challenges created by globalization and rising consumerism?

REFERENCES

Anderson, R.A. and McDaniel, R.R. (2000) Managing health care organizations: where professionalism meets complexity science. *Health Care Management Review*, 25(1): 83–92.

Anderson, R.M. and Funnell, M.M. (2005) Patient empowerment: reflections on the challenge of fostering the adoption of a new paradigm. *Patient Education and Counseling*, 57: 153–157.

Brown, J.J. and Evens, R.G. (2000) Public policy: the case for lobbying in radiology. *Radiology*, 214: 321–324.

French, W.L. and Bell, C.H. (1990) *Organization Development*. Englewood Cliffs: Prentice-Hall.

Garvin, D.A. (1993) Building a learning organization. *HBR* (July–August): 78–91.

Greer, A.L. (1988) The state of the art versus the state of the science. The diffusion of new medical technologies into practice. *International Journal of Technology Assessment and Health Care*, 4: 5–26.

Grol, R. and Grimshaw, J. (2003) From best evidence to best practice: effective implementation of change in patients' care. *Lancet*, 362: 1225–1230.

Hastings, G. and McDermott, L. (2006) Putting social marketing into practice. *British Medical Journal*, 332: 1210–1212.

Koelen, M.A. and Lindström, B. (2005) Making healthy choices easy choices: the role of empowerment. *European Journal of Clinical Nutrition*, 59 (Suppl. 1): S10–S16.

Kotler, P., Roberto, N. and Lee, N. (2002) *Social marketing: improving the quality of life*. Thousand Oaks: Sage.

Landzelius, K. (2006) The incubation of a social movement? Preterm babies, parent activists, and neonatal productions in the US context. *Social Science and Medicine*, 62: 668–682.

Miles, R. and Snow, C. (1992) Causes of failure in network organisations. *California Management Review,* 34: 53–72.

Milward, H.B. and Provan, K.G. (2003) Managing networks effectively. Paper presented at the National Public Management Research Conference, Georgetown University, Washington DC, 9–11 October.

National Social Marketing Centre (2006) *It's our health! Realising the potential of effective social marketing.* London: National Consumer Council.

Nukuro, E. (2000) The lobbying process and building advocacy networks. Paper presented at the IPPF advocacy and gender awareness workshop, Lautoka, Fiji Islands, April.

Plsek, P.E. and Greenhalgh, T. (2001) The challenge of complexity in health care. *British Medical Journal,* 323: 625–628.

Prochaska, J.O., Norcross, J.C. and DiClemente, C.C. (1994) *Changing for good.* New York: Avon.

Rosenau, P.V. (1994) Health politics meets post-modernism: its meaning and implications for community health organizing. *Journal of Health Politics, Policy and Law,* 19: 303–333.

Salamon, L.M. (2002) *The tools of government: a guide to the new governance.* New York: Oxford University Press.

Secretary of State for Health (2004) *Choosing health: making healthy choices easier.* Cm 6374. London: HMSO.

Senge, P.M. (1990) *The fifth discipline: the art and practice of the learning organisation.* London: Random House Business Books.

Sharp, L.F. and Priesmeyer, H.R. (1995) Tutorial: chaos theory – a primer for health care. *Quality Management in Health Care,* 3(4): 71–86.

Tarrow, S. (1994) *Power in movement: collective action, social movements and politics.* Cambridge: Cambridge University Press.

Tilly, C. (2004) *Social movements.* Boulder: Paradigm Publishers.

Tuohy, C.H. (2003) Agency, contract and governance: shifting shapes of accountability in the health care arena. *Journal of Health Politics Policy and Law,* 28: 195–215.

Wallerstein, N. (1992) Powerlessness, empowerment and health: implications for health promotion programs. *American Journal of Health Promotion,* 6: 197–205.

World Health Organization (WHO) (1986) *Ottawa charter for health promotion.* Copenhagen: World Health Organization.

Chapter 5

Information needs for managing for health

John Wilkinson and Kathryn Bailey

KEY POINTS OF THIS CHAPTER

- Timely, accurate and relevant information is required for public health planning and monitoring
- A central tenet of measuring health status or need is that any vital event should be related to the population and the time it occurs
- Collecting and disseminating information to optimal effect is essential for public health
- Data, information and intelligence, though used interchangeably, have different meanings
- The need in future is for more data literate managers

INTRODUCTION

Timely, accurate and relevant information is required for appropriate public health planning and monitoring in order to ensure that improved health outcomes are achieved and maintained. This chapter reviews the state of play in respect of information for public health and how it can be collected and disseminated to optimal effect. We concentrate on information for England, making reference to similar sources for Wales, Scotland and Ireland where these are available. We also touch on international data, especially those from Europe.

The information needs for managing health are very wide. In this chapter we range from information on the population – which is very important from a public health point of view and often involves data not exclusively from the health sector — to information that includes data on health services and the provision of health care.

The idea of responsibility for the health of geographically defined populations, and not just of those individuals seeking help, has been a unique strength of the British National Health Service (NHS) since its establishment in 1948 (Donaldson and Donaldson 2003). National, regional and local frameworks for the provision of health improvement and health care ensure that services are made available to local populations on the basis of their health needs. But measuring health need is not straightforward and a range of data types are used, some as direct measures and some as proxies, to illustrate different aspects of a population's health. A central tenet of measuring health status or health need is that any vital event or health-related occurrence should be related to the population and the time at which it occurs.

DATA, INFORMATION AND INTELLIGENCE

'Data', 'information' and 'intelligence' are terms that are often used interchangeably, but have very different meanings. Data are the raw numbers, sometimes rates or calculated data. Data become information when they are usable for decision-making. Intelligence usually describes the much broader concept of 'enhanced understanding' about a particular topic. It might for example include soft information and evidence from a wide range of sources.

WHY DO YOU NEED INFORMATION?

Prior to the government's comprehensive spending review in 2002, Derek Wanless, a former director of the National Westminster Bank and an economist by background, was asked by the Chancellor of the Exchequer, the government's finance minister, to examine future health trends and to identify the factors determining the long-term financial and resource needs of the NHS up until 2020 (Wanless 2002). In April 2003, he was invited to undertake a second review to provide an update of the challenges involved in achieving his 'fully engaged scenario', and in particular, on the public health challenges (Wanless 2004).

In his second report, Wanless described health data as being essential for monitoring the health of the population and for evaluating the effect of health interventions. He lamented the dearth of information on behavioural factors such as smoking, drinking and exercise, noting that, at a local level, there is no regular mechanism for a primary care trust (PCT) or local authority to gather information on its own population. He concluded that the information held about individual patients was inadequate to provide local comprehensive information on health status.

TYPES OF INFORMATION

Following publication of the government's policy statement, *Building trust in statistics*, the concept of 'National Statistics' was developed in the UK to provide a statistical service that is open and responsive to society's needs and the public agenda, and official statistics that command public confidence (HM Treasury 1999). Data deemed to be 'National Statistics' provide an up-to-date, comprehensive and meaningful description of the UK's economy and society. They must meet certain criteria; for example, they should be fit for purpose, methodologically sound, politically independent, transparently produced, and comply with the professional principles and standards set out in the National Statistics Code of Practice (Office for National Statistics 2002). All data sources covered in this section are National Statistics.

In November 2005, the Chancellor of the Exchequer announced that the Office for National Statistics would become an independent body. This is seen as an attempt by government to increase public confidence in national statistics.

Data from the decennial census

The population census – a periodic count of the number and characteristics of people living in a given geographical area – is a fundamental vehicle for the collection of population data. Coordinated by the Office for National Statistics (ONS), a census has been carried out in the United Kingdom every ten years since 1801, except for 1941; the legal authority to hold such censuses is enshrined in the 1920 Census Act. The twentieth Census was conducted on 29 April 2001 to provide a count of all persons in households in the United Kingdom. Data collected at the 2001 Census include: sex, age, marital status, country of birth, relationship of persons in household, location on census night, usual address, ethnic group, religion, health status, limiting long-term illness, accommodation type, accommodation tenure, higher qualifications, economic activity, hours worked, occupation, business or employer, workplace, journey to work, car access.

The Census provides statistical information at various population levels that is used to support the planning of public services, including health, education and transport, and for research.

Data from the 2001 Census are available in tabular form for England and Wales through National Statistics (http://www.statistics.gov.uk/census2001/), for Scotland through the General Register Office for Scotland (http://www.scrol.gov.uk/scrol/common/home.jsp), and for Northern Ireland through the Northern Ireland Statistics and Research Agency (http://www.nicensus2001.gov.uk/nica/common/home.jsp). Academics can access census data through services such as MIMAS (http://www.mimas.ac.uk/) and CASweb (http://www.census.ac.uk/casweb/). There are also commercial data handling and geographical classification packages for the analysis of census data.

101

Population data

Populations are constantly changing as individuals die, are born, and move into and out of areas. Managers and planners for health and related services are therefore unlikely to rely on descriptions of the population measured only every ten years, and details are needed about the size, shape and characteristics of the population between census points.

Population estimates – produced annually by the ONS – describe the age and sex structure of various geographic levels of population in England and Wales on 30 June each year. The latest series of population estimates (mid-2001 onwards) are based on the 2001 Census and relate to the usually resident population (i.e., they relate to where people usually live).

Population estimates are made using the *cohort component method*, which is as follows. The starting point for the estimate is the resident population on 30 June in the previous year. This population, by single year of age, is then aged by one year. Babies born during the 12-month period are added to the population and all those who have died during the 12-month period are removed according to their age, sex, and their usual place of residence. Since the registration of births and deaths is a legal requirement in the UK (see pp. 103–104), these parts of the estimation process are reasonably accurate. The other factor to be taken into account in estimating the national population is the movement of people in and out of the UK (international migration). When estimating the population of sub-national areas, movements within the UK (internal migration) must also be accounted for. Migration is the most difficult part of the population estimate process to estimate precisely, as migration is not registered in the UK, either at the national or local level. The best proxy data available on a nationally consistent basis are used to estimate migration.

Population estimates are currently produced for:

- the UK as a whole and England, Wales, Scotland and Northern Ireland separately by sex and single year of age;
- government office regions, counties, unitary authorities and local government districts in England and unitary authorities in Wales by sex and five-year age group or broad age group (children, working age and older people);
- health areas in England and Wales (health authorities in England and local health boards in Wales) by sex and five-year age group or broad age group;
- legal marital status for England and Wales as a whole;
- population estimates by primary care organization in England by sex and five-year age group or broad age group.

A number of projects are underway to improve the quality, timeliness and availability of population estimate data. These include projects to produce small area population estimates, quarterly population estimates, and improvements in the migration elements of the estimates.

In the long term, the ONS has proposed the development of an integrated population statistics system that combines census, survey, and administrative data, linked at individual person level, to create a single, comprehensive population statistics database that is updated over time (Office for National Statistics 2003). This database would be implemented in 2011 to underpin all ONS population and social statistics. This would produce significantly improved, more consistent statistics for the government community, the health service, academia, and the private sector, including more frequent, timely and accurate small area statistics; better under-standing of the groups who make up our society; and of issues such as health, crime and education and the relationships between them; improved planning, delivery and monitoring of services and better targeted resources.

Details of current methodology and projects related to population statistics can be found at <http://www.statistics.gov.uk/about/data/methodology/specific/population/default.asp>.

Vital events

Within the UK, it is a legal requirement to register vital events (births, deaths, marriages and civil partnerships). The registration service for England and Wales was established in 1837 and is the responsibility of the General Register Office (http://www.gro.gov.uk/). Equivalent organizations in other parts of the UK are the General Register Office for Scotland (http://gro-scotland.gov.uk/) and the General Register Office (Northern Ireland) (http://www.groni.gov.uk/).

The General Register Office has commissioned a project to modernize vital events information through the digitization of vital events (DoVE). The aim of the project is to scan, digitize, undertake data capture and produce an index of all birth, death and marriage records from 1837 to the present day. The outcome in 2007/08 will be a modern system of registration information and help to streamline the certificate production process.

Births data

In the UK, all births must be registered within 42 days of the birth. Stillbirths (babies born after the 24th week of pregnancy who did not show any signs of life at any time after being born) must also be registered within 42 days of the birth; registra-tion requires a medical certificate of stillbirth issued by the attending doctor or midwife.

The ONS compiles demographic statistics on births derived from the records of live and stillbirth registration within England and Wales. Variables analysed include mother's age, father's age, occurrence inside/outside marriage, social class, place of confinement, country of birth, multiple maternities and area of usual residence. The data are also used to produce conceptions statistics.

103

Statistics are produced for a range of geographies, including government office regions, county/unitary authority, local authority districts, and health areas. Not all of the above data items are available for all of these area levels.

Deaths data

In the UK, all deaths must be registered within five days of the death; registration requires a medical certificate of cause of death issued by the doctor treating the person who dies.

The ONS compiles mortality statistics that are based on registrations of deaths. Main analyses of mortality data are by age, sex, area of residence and cause of death.

Statistics are produced for a range of geographies, including government office regions, county/unitary authority, local authority districts and health areas.

HEALTH

Health Survey for England

The Health Survey for England, started in 1991, comprises an annual series of surveys. Each year the survey differs slightly by focusing on different groups in the population. The survey aims to:

- provide annual data about the nation's health;
- estimate the proportion of the population with specific health conditions;
- estimate the prevalence of risk factors associated with those conditions;
- assess the frequency with which combinations of risk factors occur;
- examine differences between population sub-groups;
- monitor targets in the health strategy;
- measure (from 1995) the height of children at different ages, replacing the national study of health and growth.

Initially the survey was undertaken by the Office of Population Censuses and Surveys (later to become the Office of National Statistics – ONS), but it is now carried out by the Joint Survey Unit of the National Centre for Social Research and the Department of Epidemiology and Public Health at University College London.

The survey combines a series of questions administered by a trained interviewer and also, more importantly, some direct measurements that are carefully standardized (e.g., blood tests, measurement of height and weight, electrocardiogram (ECG) reading, and lung function tests).

There are some topics that are covered every year, these are:

- general health and psycho-social indicators;
- smoking;
- alcohol;
- demographic and socio-economic indicators;
- use of health services and prescribed medicines – the focus for these may vary from year to year to suit the modular content of the survey;
- measurement of height, weight and blood pressure.

In addition there is a separate module, which differs from year to year; the following topics have been covered in recent years:

1993: cardiovascular disease;
1994: cardiovascular disease;
1995: asthma, accidents, disability;
1996: asthma, accidents, special measures of general health (Euroqol, SF36);
1997: children and young people;
1998: cardiovascular disease;
1999: ethnic groups;
2000: older people, social exclusion;
2001: respiratory disease, atopic conditions, disability and non-fatal accidents;
2002: children and young people and infants and their mothers;
2003: cardiovascular risk factors;
2004: childhood obesity and ethnic minorities.

The survey covers only a small sample of the population, but this varies from year to year. Thus in 1991 and 1992 the sample size was only 3,000, but in 1998 the sample size was 16,000 adults and 4,000 children. Increasing the sample size enables further conclusions to be drawn from the survey, for example at a regional level or by socio-economic groups. However, the size of the survey means that useful information can only be drawn at relatively large population sizes. Normally results have been published at national and regional level only, but in recent years results at former strategic health authority levels have also been published.

Results from the Health Survey for England (HSE) are published mainly in the form of paper reports, though much material is now available from the website (via the Department of Health website). In addition, raw data can be obtained with permission for appropriate purposes from the data archive in Essex (University of Essex 2006).

One of the problems in using HSE data is that they are only published at regional and strategic health authority level. This means that obtaining data at PCT or local authority level is not possible because of the size of the sample. In some areas, proposals are being developed to 'boost' the sample size of the HSE to provide data at this level. Although potentially expensive, this is a good option as the HSE is a well validated instrument and will provide sound, consistent results.

Registers

The NHS Modernization Agency Coronary Heart Disease Collaborative stated:

> An accurate disease register enables the provision of a systematic, evidence based approach to the care of patients with a specific health problem. When the register has been developed and is adequately maintained it will facilitate effective audit of appropriate patient care and allow timely recall for monitoring purposes. Practices will be able to easily retrieve accurate information for their quarterly team meetings, as described in the Coronary Heart Disease National Service Framework. A well developed and maintained disease register is central and crucial to provision of quality care in general practice.
>
> (NHS Modernization Agency 2002: 12)

A number of registers are currently in existence in the United Kingdom, which may provide information on health. Unfortunately, the only comprehensive registers on health are cancer registries, which will be considered later. There are a number of other registries, but none can currently provide a national picture. A list of registers held on health is shown in Box 5.1.

BOX 5.1 EXAMPLES OF REGISTERS CURRENTLY HELD ON DISEASE AREAS IN THE UK

Heart disease registers
Held by general practitioners to facilitate the management and surveillance of patients with heart disease and related problems.

Diabetic Registers
Originally held at hospital level, many then developed into district diabetes registers to provide a comprehensive picture of diabetes in an area.

Renal Registry
The UK Renal Registry collects and analyses data from renal units relating to the incidence, clinical management and outcomes of renal disease to provide a source of comparative data for audit, planning, clinical governance and research. The UK Renal Registry covers 85 per cent of renal units in England and 100 per cent of renal units in Wales; the Scottish Renal Registry covers 100 per cent of renal units in Scotland.

Registers tend to be held at different levels in the population. Some are held at general practice level while others are maintained at larger population levels, such as PCT level. Yet other registries are maintained at regional and national levels.

Registers have a number of uses. They can be used to study the amount of disease in a society, and trends. Registers such as cancer registers can play an important role in monitoring the effect of various types of treatment or other interventions. They can also be crucial for the planning of services. However, registers are only of use if they are as accurate as possible. Running and maintaining any sort of register is an immensely costly and time-consuming process.

Cancer registration

Cancer registries have been in existence in the United Kingdom for over forty years. They collect data on all cases of cancer in the country and, as such, are one of the few sources of comprehensive data on the health of the population. There are nine cancer registries in England, one in Scotland (coordinated by the Information and Statistics Division of NHS Scotland), one in Wales, and one in Northern Ireland.

Cancer registries submit data to the national cancer intelligence centre at the Office of National Statistics, which then collates the data to produce a national picture. Data can then be compared internationally.

Cancer registries are crucial in measuring the impact of cancer on health, and on health policies in improving the outcomes from cancer. The NHS Cancer Plan seeks to improve the outcome following treatment for cancer in England, and only through cancer registries can this be effectively monitored.

The functions of registries at a regional level are to collect data, and analyse and disseminate information from these data. One of the features of cancer registries is the multiple sources of ascertainment. Although there is no one uniform system, a cancer registry record is usually triggered from a pathology report, as most cancers are likely to be biopsied at an early stage and, therefore, the first indication to the system that there is a cancer is likely to be via a pathology report. Cancer registries in England are now in the process of implementing electronic data capture, but in a number of regions these data are captured by data clerks employed either by the hospital or operating peripatetically from the cancer registry. In the paper system, a clerk visiting the hospital will have a first notification about a patient with cancer; he or she will then complete a standardized form, which is then used at the cancer registry to augment the first notification of a new cancer patient. Data will be collected on the precise tumour pathology, the site of the cancer, the morphology (cell type) of the cancer, the date of first presentation, any subsequent treatment and death. The cancer registry increasingly will be interested to collect staging data. Of course, basic demographic data about the patient is also collected at the same time.

The Department of Health lists the following functions of cancer registries:

- monitoring trends in cancer incidence, prevalence and survival over time and by different areas and social groups;
- evaluating the effectiveness of cancer prevention and screening programmes – e.g., monitoring the effectiveness of the existing national screening programmes for breast and cervical cancer, and informing the design of new programmes for colorectal and ovarian cancer screening;
- evaluating the quality and outcomes of cancer care by providing comparative data about treatment patterns and outcomes;
- evaluating the impact of environmental and social factors on cancer risk; for example, cancer registry data are used to investigate possible cancer risks in relation to power lines, landfill sites and mobile phones, and they are also used to investigate differences in cancer incidence, survival and access to treatment between social groups and thus contribute to programmes aimed at reducing inequalities in health outcomes;
- supporting investigations into the causes of cancer;
- providing information in support of cancer genetic counselling services for individuals and families at higher risk of developing cancer.

In recent years, in a growing climate of concerns about patient confidentiality, the whole process of cancer registration has been put under threat. Cancer registries collect named patient data. It has always been argued that it is essential to have a name to ensure that any record is properly constructed (e.g. contains information about the same individual – a potential problem when data are coming from a variety of sources). Data from the cancer registries are never published at individual level (or identifiable level) – the privacy of the patient is always protected.

Data on risk factors

Both the second Wanless report and the English public health policy statement, *Choosing Health* (Secretary of State for Health 2004), have emphasized the paucity of good local level data on lifestyle risk factors (e.g. smoking, obesity, physical activity, diet, alcohol, and drug misuse). These are now needed to plan and monitor many important public health interventions at many geographic levels. Information on these risk factors at national and regional level mainly comes from the Health Survey for England and the General Household Survey. However, sample sizes are too small to produce figures at local level.

Local health and lifestyle surveys provide a flexible approach to collecting lifestyle data. Many health organizations, such as primary care trusts and health authorities, have undertaken local health and lifestyle surveys that have provided valuable data for planning. However, these have rarely been undertaken more than once or twice in a decade in each area. Additionally, they have not usually been done with comparable methods in neighbouring areas. It is therefore difficult to compare results across areas and over time. In recent years response rates appear to have fallen — and are sometimes now below 50 per cent.

There are a number of potential sources of local lifestyle data, as follows:

■ *Enhanced national surveys*. For the Health Survey for England, a full or partial boost survey service is available to local organizations. To date relatively few local authorities and primary care trusts have made use of this service, but some Public Health Observatories are considering this approach within their regions.

■ *Increased local surveys*. Repeating surveys can generate valuable local trend data but requires local commitment, funding and a planned survey programme.

■ *Synthetic estimates*. The prevalence of lifestyle risk factors in local populations and sub-groups within local populations can be estimated by modelling and extrapolation of prevalence data from national surveys. In principle synthetic estimates could be generated for a range of lifestyle factors and different geographies.

■ *Commercial data*. A number of commercial organizations offer lifestyle data derived from consumer surveys designed primarily to inform marketing. Topics vary but include questions on the purchase or consumption of tobacco, food and alcohol.

■ *Primary care data sources*. There is increasingly systematic recording of lifestyle data in primary care, particularly in patients with diabetes, coronary heart disease and other conditions where lifestyle data may be particularly relevant.

The different potential sources of lifestyle data all have different comparative strengths and weaknesses. It is extremely unlikely that any one source will provide all of the solutions to all of the lifestyle surveillance challenges faced by local organizations. The Association of Public Health Observatories has produced a technical briefing that outlines the suitability of the different data sources for local-level surveillance of smoking, obesity, diet, physical activity, alcohol consumption, and multiple risk factors (Association of Public Health Observatories 2005).

HEALTH SERVICES

Primary Care

Since general practitioners (GPs) are responsible for both providing care services and referring on for secondary and specialist care services, the medical records held by GPs potentially provide a rich source of data that could be used to monitor health services, measure the quality of care and undertake population-based research

(Gnani and Majeed 2006). In 2002, the government launched the National Programme for Information Technology (NPfIT), now rebadged Connecting for Health, with the aim of producing a data spine with a cradle-to-grave NHS record for each patient. In 2005, the Health and Social Care Information centre was established to combine the information systems for health and social care and to provide national leadership for data and information to support the NHS. Before these national initiatives, good use of data from primary care had been driven by local initiatives.

Patient registration systems

The Patient Registration System, a major component of the National Health Application and Infrastructure Services (NHAIS), also known as the 'Exeter System', is one of the largest population databases in operation. It contains demographic details of some 60 million patients registered with NHS GPs. The central index of patient registration details is held by the National Health Service Central Register (NHSCR) based at Southport. Electronic interchange of data between health authorities and NHSCR helps to reduce duplicate entries and inaccurate registrations.

The system allows for a range of health services management functions such as calculation of capitation payments, screening call and recall processes, movement of medical records, and production of prescription exemption certificates. It also aids the demographic analysis of patient data by linking geographic data (based on the 1991 Census) to GP information.

Patient registrations are therefore used as a local source of population data. However, patients frequently change address without notifying their GP and sometimes patients on the list may no longer be present in the area. This creates 'list variation', which can be observed as a difference between official population estimates and estimates obtained from GP lists. These differences are particularly apparent for inner city areas.

General Medical Services and Quality and Outcomes Framework

The Quality and Outcomes Framework (QOF) is a voluntary system of financial incentives related to the new General Medical Services (GMS) contract. The aim is to reward contractors for good practice through quality improvement. QOF measures achievement against evidence-based indicators, including 76 clinical indicators in ten chronic disease areas, 56 organizational indicators, four patient experience indicators and ten additional service indicators. It aims to give objective evidence of the quality of care delivered to patients measured against national targets in the GMS contract. Achievement against each target is scored, and it is possible to compare QOF score by practice and by PCT.

Quality Management and Analysis System and Quality Prevalence and Indicator Database

Quality Management and Analysis System (QMAS) is a national web-based software tool that allows practices, primary care trusts and health authorities to measure their performance against national targets set out in the new GMS contract. The most important information collected via QMAS is on disease register size and process of care measures for chronic conditions, some of which are linked to better health outcomes. It should be noted, however, that practices are allowed to exclude some patients from the denominator for individual clinical indicators. The usefulness of QMAS in providing information on the prevalence of disease at local level is dependent upon the accuracy of practice list data, knowledge of the characteristics of the practice population and careful interpretation of exception coding.

The Quality Prevalence and Indicator Database (QPID) held by the Health and Social Care Information Centre aims to improve access to QMAS data by users in the Department of Health and the NHS.

Prescribing Analysis and Cost

Prescribing Analysis and Cost (PACT) data, administered by the Prescription Pricing Division of the NHS Business Services Authority, includes details of all dispensed NHS prescriptions. Analysed information is fed back to practices, primary care trusts, health authorities, the Department of Health, National Institute for Health and Clinical Excellence, the Healthcare Commission, the National Prescribing Centre, and the Health and Social Care Information Centre Prescribing Support Unit. Analyses of the data include:

- costs and volumes of prescribing;
- prescribing from specified formularies;
- low-income scheme index (LISI) scores, which identify the percentage of the cost of all prescriptions that is exempt on the grounds of low income;
- comparative measures for populations using a range of prescribing units (e.g., ASTRO-PU, STAR-PU).

In their current form PACT data have some limitations. Since they are not linked to demographic, clinical or diagnostic data they cannot be used to calculate age- and sex-specific prescribing rates nor can they be used to look at prescribing patterns for particular conditions.

GP Research Database

The GP Research Database was initially set up as a research tool, principally to carry out studies related to drug side effects. An anonymized longitudinal database of medical records from primary care, it is a valuable tool for research in a broad range of areas, including clinical epidemiology, disease patterns, disease management, outcomes research, and drug utilization. Since 1999, the database has been managed by the Medicines and Healthcare Products Regulatory Agency (MHRA) with the aim of improving access to the database for research purposes.

Secondary care

Data on people who are treated in hospital provide a useful indication of health need, but also, perhaps more accurately, of health service utilization. There is a long history of recording data on activity in hospitals. From 1955 to 1985, the Hospital Inpatient Enquiry (HIPE) collected data on a 10 per cent sample of those treated in hospital. This was then followed in the late 1960s by Hospital Activity Analysis (HAA), which sought to collect data on all patients treated as inpatients in hospital. Over the years, the quality of data has improved enormously. In the early years of HAA much of the data regarding hospital treatment was incomplete and inaccurate.

The advent of the internal market in the 1990s in England, when the then government introduced market-style competition into the NHS, meant hospitals had a much greater incentive to record activity accurately as these data were important for how much they were paid. Of course, where there was a particular national focus on targets and waiting lists – for example, on hip, knee, and cataract operations – the data were much better.

Hospital Episode Statistics

Hospital Episode Statistics (HES) currently collect over 50 million records per year and is an enormous database. This includes data for admitted patients (inpatients), outpatients, and accidents and emergencies routinely exchanged between providers of health care for NHS patients in England and the commissioners of the care. Health care providers collect administrative and clinical information to support patient care. The data are then submitted to the NHS Wide Clearing Service (NWCS), which, as well as forwarding it to the commissioners, also copies the information to a database. At specified times during the year, the NWCS takes an extract from their database and sends it to HES and so HES data are fixed whilst data on the NWCS continue to change.

The data are validated and cleaned, and then made available through the HES data warehouse. Validation and cleaning includes:

- check-in reports describing the quality and completeness of received data;
- autocleaning to check fields for missing and invalid data items;
- addition of derived items.

There is increased interest in making use of clearing service data, which has the advantage of being timely but the disadvantage of being 'uncleaned', unvalidated, and potentially incomplete.

Other data sources from hospitals

There are many databases held within hospitals. Some are small local systems, others are part of national systems. Other major data sources from hospitals include outpatient data and data from the accident and emergency departments.

Better Metrics

The Better Metrics project arose from a general concern that clinicians were not engaged by targets and indicators used to assess performance in the NHS (Healthcare Commission 2006). For example, local clinicians were not always aware of the targets being measured, or the components of their organization's (then) star rating indicators, and were unlikely to be using them as part of their service quality improvement initiatives. One possible explanation for this was that some of the existing performance measures were not sufficiently relevant to clinicians' day-to-day practice, or to the patients they were treating. In January 2004, the project was launched to develop more clinically relevant measures of performance. These measures were termed 'metrics' to avoid confusion with other terms such as targets, indicators or benchmarks. The aim was that the proposed 'metrics' could be used for any of these purposes. The project also aimed to produce some criteria for what makes a 'good metric', to assist local services in developing their own.

Metrics are available for cancer, heart disease and stroke, children and maternity, diabetes, emergency care, health inequalities, learning disabilities, long-term neurological conditions, mental health, older people, patient experience, primary care, and R&D. Metrics for renal services and ambulance services are expected shortly. Information about the project can be found at <http://www.osha.nhs.uk/>.

NON-HEALTH DATA WITH IMPLICATIONS FOR HEALTH

Good health depends on a number of factors not just the quality of health services. Some of these factors are considered in this section.

Socio-economic status

Socio-economic status is the single greatest determinant at population level of health status throughout life. In the absence of routine information on income, expenditure and wealth proxy measures are used to indicate the socio-economic position of people living in specific geographical areas. A range of so-called 'deprivation indices' exist as proxies for socio-economic status (Carr-Hill and Chalmers-Dixon 2005). The index in most common use at present is the Index of Multiple Deprivation (IMD) 2004 (Office of the Deputy Prime Minister 2004).

Socio-economic status is intimately related to income and employment, although unemployment has been shown to have an effect on health that is independent of poverty. Data on employment, unemployment and uptake of benefits related to unemployment or inability to work can be accessed from NOMIS (http://www.nomisweb.co.uk).

Education

Developing skills and gaining qualifications is beneficial for mental health, bolstering self-esteem, establishing self-identity, and improves employment opportunity and earning potential. Position within the labour market and life chances are largely determined by educational attainment.

Information on educational attainment during school key stages has been available for some time for each school and local education authority from the Department for Education and Skills (http://www.dfes.gov.uk). More recently, educational attainment for pupils resident in a range of geographic areas has been released on the Neighbourhood Statistics website (http://neighbourhood.statistics.gov.uk/dissemination/). Information on basic literacy and numeracy skills in adults is available from the Basic Skills Agency (http://www.basic-skills.co.uk).

Housing

Having adequate shelter is a prerequisite for health; lack of housing and living in poor quality housing are related to disadvantage and poor health. Information on housing tenure and the condition of housing stock is available from the Department for Communities and Local Government (http://www.communities.gov.uk/).

Crime

Crime and fear of crime can profoundly affect the quality of people's lives. Recorded crime statistics for Crime and Disorder Reduction Partnership areas (which are coterminous with local authorities) are available from the Home Office (http://www.homeoffice.gov.uk).

Transport

Transport, which includes walking and cycling, as well as the use of private vehicles, public transport and goods vehicles, can have a wide range of beneficial and deleterious effects on health. Positive effects include recreation, exercise, and access to employment, education, shops, recreation, social support networks, health services and the countryside. Negative effects include pollution, traffic injuries, noise, stress and anxiety, danger, and community severance (Transport and Health Study Group 2003). Transport statistics are available from the Department for Transport (http://www.dft.gov.uk).

Environmental quality

There are close links between the environment and people's health. A high-quality environment enables people to live longer in good health. Environmental problems such as pollution and flooding can pose significant risks to health. The relationships between pollution, the environment and health are often complex, and a greater understanding is needed of the links between exposure to pollution and the effect it has on health, as well as the impacts on health of mixtures of chemicals, microbes or physical changes in the environment. Statistics on environmental quality are available from the Department for Environment, Food and Rural Affairs (http://www.defra.gov.uk).

DATA FROM EUROPE

There has been growing interest in looking at data from Europe (and indeed beyond) in recent years to gain a better understanding of health. The Treaty of Amsterdam signalled a new public health competency for the European Union (European Union 1997). Health information is a major strand of the work of DG Sanco (Directorate of Health and Consumer Affairs) of the EU and can be accessed from <http://www.ec.europa.eu/health-eu/index_en.htm>. This competency is backed up by a significant level of funding, which is available to support relevant public health projects in the EU. Within the UK, health communities are increasingly interested in making comparisons between their areas and comparable areas of Europe. The advent of major structural funds available to regions has further stimulated interest in activities in Europe. The provision of health care, however, remains firmly a responsibility of member states.

Eurostat

Eurostat is the European Union's statistical service based in Luxemburg. Eurostat collates a wide range of statistics from European Union members and selected data from EFTA countries (Iceland, Norway and Liechtenstein). Data collected on health is but one aspect of Eurostat's work (European Union 2004).

The data on health can be classified into three groups:

■ mortality data;
■ data on health care;
■ health status.

Mortality data

The medical certification of death is a requirement of all member states and enables mortality patterns across the European Union to be determined. As a minimum, data are collected on age, sex, and cause of death. Death is classified using the 'European shortlist' of causes of death (International Statistical Classification of Diseases and Related problems (ICD)). Other agencies, such as the World Health Organization, also collate data on death.

In order to make meaningful comparisons between countries it is necessary to take account of the age and sex structure of the population. This is known as the process of standardization. There are two main methods of standardization: direct and indirect. These methods can be explored in detail in standard epidemiological texts. Very often data are standardized to the European standard population, which is a theoretical population used for such calculations.

Health care data

Data on health care are collected less comprehensively than death data. The two main groups of data collected under this category are on resources used in health care (people and facilities). People include doctors, nurses, midwives; resources include hospitals, beds. Most countries have a clear understanding of what constitutes a doctor, and this is a profession which is very tightly regulated across the world. However, other professional groups present more complexity. For example, the classification of a nurse may differ in countries.

Hospital beds are a traditional but rather inadequate way of describing health care facilities.

Data on patient contacts vary from country to country. For example, most countries collect data on hospital inpatients, but again that may differ according to the definition of a hospital, clinic, and so on. In many countries, data on outpatients are not collected. Similarly, the collection of data from accident and emergency departments is variable. Certain types of data are collected very well (e.g. transplantation rates). In some countries data on certain sensitive areas is collected very variably (e.g. abortion rates).

Other sources of data include the European Community Household Panel. This was established in 1994 by Eurostat, and has led to a huge dataset that can provide comparisons between countries of the European Union. Thus recent reports include studies on unemployment, poverty and deprivation in Europe.

116

The labour force survey is undertaken by the Office of National Statistics every three months and is a sample survey of households living at private addresses in Great Britain. The survey collects information on individuals' personal circumstances and their labour market status during a specific reference period (usually one week). It is carried out under a European Union directive and uses internationally agreed definitions and concepts.

Eurobarometer is a series of public opinion surveys carried out in countries of the European Union at least twice a year. Since the 1970s they have provided regular monitoring of social and public attitudes in Europe.

Data on health care facilities are also collected by the WHO (World Health Organization) and the OECD (Organization for Economic Co-operation and Development).

Health status data

This area of data is much more poorly collected than the other two areas; it includes:

- anthropometric data (height, weight, BMI, etc.);
- lifestyle data (smoking, exercise, alcohol consumption, etc.);
- self-perceived health;
- disability;
- morbidity (main disease for which data are available at EU level – e.g. cancers, infectious diseases, Aids);
- DFLE (disease free life expectancy) or healthy life years expectancy (HLYE);
- averages, percentages, absolute numbers, incidence rates (crude and standardized).

Sources: SILC (Survey on Income and Living Conditions), HIS (Health Information System) and new EHIS (European Health Information System), Eurobarometer, other organizations (IARC, EuroHIV, EuroTB).

All data from Eurostat are now provided free and can be downloaded from the Eurostat website (http://epp.eurostat.cec.eu.int./).

European Community Health Indicators

The European Community Health Indicators (ECHI) project was carried out as part of the Health Monitoring Programme and the Community Public Health Programme 2003–2008 of the European Union. The result of the project is a list of 'indicators' for the public health field.

The first set of ECHI indicators includes 40 items organized into four domains as follows:

- demographic and socio-economic factors (eight indicators);
- health status (14 indicators);

117

- determinants of health (five indicators);
- health interventions and services (13 indicators).

Indicators are reasonably comparable between member states, assessment of comparability having been undertaken by Eurostat. Indicators have been stratified by gender and age where this was considered useful or appropriate. Indicator data are available from <http://europa.ec.europa.eu/health/ph_information/dissemination/echi/echi_en.htm>.

Indicateurs sante des régions dans Europe

The Indicateurs sante des régions dans Europe (ISARE) project developed out of a desire to be able to compare data at a sub-national level as well as at a national level. The project was coordinated by the Federation of French Health Observatories (FNORS) within the framework of the Health Monitoring Programme from the European Commission.

The first phase, ISARE I (1999–2001), focused on identifying, for each country, the most appropriate sub-national level ('health region') for the exchange of health indicators within the European Union. Availability of data at those levels was also assessed.

The second phase, ISARE II (2002–2004), tested the feasibility of collecting regional health data in each European country. This involved defining indicators, collecting data, creating a database and testing comparability.

A third phase of the project, ISARE III, is now underway; this aims to repeat the earlier ISARE I and II projects to include all the 25 European Union countries plus Switzerland and Norway. This work will report in 2006. All the projects are reported on the ISARE website (http://www.isare.org).

WORLD HEALTH ORGANIZATION

Health data from Europe and internationally

The World Health Organization (WHO) is the United Nations specialized health agency set up in 1948. The WHO operates from six regional offices. The European office, based in Denmark, covers a total of 52 countries from Norway to Uzbekistan. The WHO statistical information system (WHOSIS – http://www3.who.int/whosis/core/core_select.cfm) provides a range of health-related epidemiological and statistical information. In addition, there are often specific data available from particular health programmes.

The WHO produces core health indicators for each of the 192 member countries and includes data on mortality in adults and children, population growth rate, fertility rate, years of healthy life lost, life expectancy, and government expenditure on health.

The European office of WHO provides further statistical data on health in the region.

European 'Health for All' database (HFA-DB)

The European 'Health for All' database (HFA-DB) provides easy and rapid access to a wide range of basic health statistics for the 52 member states of the WHO European region (http://www.euro.who.int/hfadb).

European mortality indicators (HFA-MDB)

The European mortality indicators database (HFA-MDB) provides mortality indicators for 67 different causes of death, split by age and sex.

European computerized information system for infectious diseases (CISID)

The centralized information system for infectious diseases (CISID) uses advanced technology to collect, analyse and present data on infectious diseases in the WHO European Region (http://data.euro.who.int/CISID/).

European alcohol control database

The alcohol control database provides data to track and assess alcohol policies and their implementation within and across countries of the European region (http://data.euro.who.int/alcohol/).

European tobacco control database

The tobacco control database contains data on smoking prevalence and various aspects of tobacco control policies in European countries. It provides standardized information to track and assess the tobacco-related situation within and across countries (http://data.euro.who.int/tobacco/).

Risk factors for non-communicable diseases in Europe

Offers data on the prevalence of main risk factors of major non-communicable diseases and lifestyle-related conditions in selected countries, based on health surveys of population samples and collected within the framework of the WHO countrywide integrated non-communicable diseases intervention (CINDI) programme (http://www.euro.who.int/InformationSources/Data/20010828_5).

119

PRESENTING INFORMATION AND DISSEMINATION

Appropriate knowledge, skills and systems are required to turn data into useful information. Public health information specialists have a wide-ranging knowledge of different datasets and skills in presentation of information. They should also have a good understanding of the context and limitations of health-related data so that they can interpret and present information in a meaningful way.

There is some evidence that managers of health systems have been used to operating in an information-free zone for many years. Relevant data and information in a useful format has not been available, so managers have become used to making decisions in the absence of good-quality data. There are a number of reasons why this is likely to change in the future. The increasing involvement of the private sector in the provision of health care means that a new standard of business case for future development is required. This means that information at a level not previously seen is required in business cases. Therefore managers will need to become much more literate in the use of health information.

Data and information are available to those working in the health service in a range of formats. The most common are outlined below.

Indicator sets

For the non-specialist, indicator sets are a common way of making available pre-analysed information. They are often accompanied by visualization tools to help with interpretation. Examples of indicator sets are given in Box 5.2.

Reports

Focused reports remain a good way of presenting information to managers and decision-makers. The Office for National Statistics publishes a range of population- and health-related data through a number of annual publications (e.g. *annual review of the Registrar General on deaths in England and Wales* (DH1), *Births and patterns of family building in England and Wales* (FM1)), or quarterly publications (e.g. *Population Trends* and *Health Statistics Quarterly*).

Public Health Observatories publish reports on a range of health topics, making effective use of different sources of data and information. Through their national association, Public Health Observatories produce and publish the *Collection of reports on indications of public health in the English regions* (Association of Public Health Observatories 2006). The Indications series includes a central set of indicators supplemented by a series of topic-based reports that provide a summary of progress towards delivery of public health priorities at regional level. This project uses a number of well-recognized tools for the analysis and presentation of the data, including a balanced scorecard approach, control charts or funnel plots for visual display and traffic lights to highlight areas worthy of further investigation.

BOX 5.2   EXAMPLES OF INDICATOR SETS RELATED TO HEALTH

Compendium of Clinical and Health Indicators

Commissioned by the Department of Health to bring together indicators from several data sets developed over a number of years in response to a variety of needs and policy initiatives (e.g., Public Health Common Data Set, Population Health Outcome Indicators, Our Healthier Nation Indicators, clinical indicators, cancer survival indicators, and others. The indicators cover various aspects of population health and clinical and health outcome. Available from <www.nchod.nhs.uk> or <nww.nchod.nhs.uk>.

Local basket of inequalities indicators

Commissioned by the Department of Health to help support local action to achieve the government's national inequalities targets for life expectancy and infant mortality, by highlighting information relevant to addressing the targets and assisting local areas with monitoring progress towards reducing health inequalities. Available from: <www.lho.org.uk>.

Health poverty index

Commissioned by the Department of Health to allow groups, differentiated by geography, social or economic position and cultural identity, to be contrasted in terms of their 'health poverty'. A group's 'health poverty' is a combination of both its present state of health and its future health potential or lack of it. Available from <www.hpi.org.uk>.

Health profiles

The Public Health Observatories were commissioned to produce a health profile for every local authority in England. These profiles comprise a set of 30 health indicators, which were published in June 2006. The aim of this project, which was signalled in the White Paper *Choosing Health* was to produce a consistent set of indicators at local authority level that will be updated each year. Available from <http://www.communityhealthprofiles.info/index.php>.

Websites

Access to health-related data and information has been revolutionized by the growth of electronic media and use of information technology. The internet has become a valuable resource for providing access to data, information and reports on topics of interest.

Websites often provide a first 'port of call' when seeking health-related information. The following provide valuable sources of data and information and signpost other data providers:

- Office for National Statistics (http://www.statistics.gov.uk), including Neighbourhood Statistics (http://neighbourhood.statistics.gov.uk);
- Department of Health (http://www.dh.gov.uk);
- Clinical and Health Outcomes Knowledge Base (<http://www.nchod.nhs.uk>, <http://nww.nchod.nhs.uk>);
- Health and Social Care Information Centre (http://www.ic.nhs.uk);
- Public Health Observatories (http://www.apho.org.uk);
- Public Health Electronic Library (http://www.phel.org.uk);
- National Institute for Health and Clinical Excellence (http://www.nice.org.uk);
- Healthcare Commission (http://www.healthcarecommission.org.uk).

Other dissemination issues

In recent years there has been a growing interest in making information more accessible. Although private information providers have operated in the field for many years, there has been an accelerating involvement of private sector organizations. There is a growing recognition that dissemination of information could be improved. One example is the entry into the market of a private sector organization called 'Dr Foster'. This company has been successful in entering the arena in making better use of information. Initially the organization published a number of 'good hospital guides' in national newspapers. More recently the company has expanded its activities into other territories such as public health. Controversially, in 2005 the new Health and Social Care Information Centre entered a commercial relationship with Dr Foster to create a new company called 'Dr Foster Intelligence'. One declared intent of the new Information Centre is to stimulate the development of a market in health intelligence with much more explicit charging for services. This could have profound effects on the way information is presented and utilized in the future. There is a suggestion that if intelligence is paid for, it is more likely to be more valued. It is likely that more private sector providers will enter the market in years to come, and entirely possible that the entirety of health information could be provided from the private sector in the future.

The development of the World Wide Web as a method of dissemination of information and intelligence is likely to continue and the demand for desktop tools to interrogate large datasets are likely to be in increased demand in years to come.

A STRATEGY FOR INFORMATION AND INTELLIGENCE

During 2006, the Department of Health in England published, for consultation, an Information and Intelligence Strategy (Department of Health 2006a). Whilst the strategy is primarily focused on supporting key priorities set out in *Choosing health* (Secretary of State for Health 2004) and *Our health, our care, our say* (Secretary of State for Health 2006), its implementation should also support wider health priorities such as tackling inequalities, health protection, and effective commissioning of health and well-being. Its aim is to improve the availability and quality of health information and intelligence across England and to increase its use to support population health improvement, health protection and work on care standards and quality. Key objectives of the strategy are to make information and knowledge available to:

- local communities to inform their decisions;
- support the work of professionals engaged in improving the health of the population;
- meet the needs of government departments for health-related policy objectives.

The strategy has a strong vision, but is currently weak on plans for implementing and achieving the vision. It is anticipated that the details of implementation can be strengthened through the process of consultation. The four main elements or work streams of the strategy are discussed below.

Improved data and information provision

This workstream is, at least initially, likely to focus on bringing together information that is already available. This will take the guise of developing indicator sets and standardized reports. The health profiles project undertaken by the Public Health Observatories is an example of this kind of work, which seeks to make existing data more widely available and more easily accessible.

Through this workstream, the strategy will seek to increase the availability of a wider range of information relevant to public health. This work includes putting in place processes to collect new data (e.g. the recently published guidance on measuring childhood obesity: Department of Health 2006b) and projects aimed at exploring the potential for use at population level of existing data sources (e.g. exploration of data on lifestyle and obesity from general practice systems). This work is to be supported by a renewed focus on data quality (starting with data on ethnicity) and effective communication, including communicating public health messages direct to the public.

Stronger organizations

This workstream tasks newly appointed Directors of Public Health for the Regions/ Strategic Health Authorities to ensure that all regional bodies with an information and intelligence function work together in a coordinated fashion to support public health and other government priorities.

In addition, this workstream seeks to address problems associated with data sharing within the NHS through the creation of an information governance specification and the creation of public health 'safe havens'. The opportunity afforded by a high degree of coterminosity between government office regions and SHAs, and the strengthening of functions at that geography, will enable much greater sharing and linkage of data. Public Health Observatories (PHOs) envisage a role in supporting local services wanting to set up data-sharing initiatives, and also expect to be safe havens in their own right. PHOs are able to demonstrate the highest level of probity and security in handling confidential data. They should have access to the same data sources with the same degree of timeliness as primary care trusts and health authorities. Removing these barriers is one way in which information services could be improved at no cost.

At national level, a number of key information and intelligence resources are being developed. The National Institute for Health and Clinical Excellence has been commissioned to undertake a full review of the effectiveness evidence for methods of achieving behaviour change at community and population level. A public health data mart and new National Library for Public Health will be developed through NHS Connecting for Health.

Workforce training and support

This workstream proposes the establishment of a Public Health Intelligence Workforce Steering Group to recommend workforce developments within the wider NHS Agenda for Change Knowledge and Skills Framework. The group will assess and recommend the information skills required in all organizations, work to improve the availability of training in this area, and develop career pathways for information staff.

New NHS organizations should give the highest priority to knowledge management – the application of knowledge from information, research and experience. Staff working at local level need to value knowledge; developing capacity and capability in information and intelligence will be crucial to the success of the strategy.

Clear and defined career pathways for information specialists are vital in developing and maintaining the capacity and capability in health information and intelligence. *Agenda for Change* has provided a good start in defining different levels within the information workforce. However, the strategy has not given sufficient emphasis to the importance of leadership roles in health intelligence. It is unfortunate that the UK Voluntary Register for Public Health Specialists does not clearly recognize public health intelligence as a sub-speciality in its competency framework even though it is possible to seek registration as a public health intelligence-defined specialist. The Public Health Intelligence Workforce Steering Group will therefore need to consider leadership roles alongside training and development.

Development of a National Health information and intelligence system

This workstream focuses on the development of the long-term vision of a central public health information system built around the NHS Connecting for Health Secondary Uses Service. This would provide a unique opportunity to bring together a wide range of data in a single secure environment with very flexible potential to provide data for public health practice and research. The work will be underpinned by the best available expertise in health informatics. However, this vision is based on an NHS-centric view and would not address the imperatives for partnership working at local level, particularly where this involves key players from outside the NHS such as local authorities and local strategic partnerships.

THE ROLE OF OBSERVATORIES

Public Health Observatories in England were set up as a result of the public health strategy, *Saving Lives: Our Healthier Nation* (Secretary of State for Health 1999). The strategy contained the expected roles of PHOs, which were described as follows:

- monitoring health and disease trends and highlighting areas for action;
- identifying gaps in health information;
- advising on methods for health and health inequality impact assessments;
- drawing together information from different sources in new ways to improve health;
- evaluating progress by local agencies in improving health and cutting inequality;
- looking ahead to give early warning of future public health problems.

They were also given a list of organizations with which they were expected to work. These included NHS organizations, and regional bodies.

Public Health Observatories owe their origin to the French, who have a penchant for establishing observatories. Over 150 observatories of one description or another exist in France. As their website states: 'if there is a problem – create an Observatory'! The first health observatory was set up in the area around Paris in the 1970s. Later observatories were set up in every region in France (including their offshore dependencies) making a total of 26 health observatories.

Hemmings and Wilkinson (2003) have described the key components of an observatory. They suggested that an observatory, in this context, has a number of features – namely, it serves to combine a number of qualities of academic departments and state-based public health departments by providing high-quality, relevant regional intelligence for those who need it. The observatories do this to a short timetable, enabling them to respond to new and rapidly developing situations. They noted that

125

observatories were often small organizations with a degree of autonomy. Observatories often hold very little data themselves and are not normally involved in their collection, but are able to access data readily, and, using a range of skills and expertise, assemble it in a way that can influence policy-makers.

SECURITY, CONFIDENTIALITY AND DISCLOSURE CONTROL

In his second report, Wanless identified current difficulties in accessing and disseminating personal information and anonymous information at low-level geographies as an important issue undermining not only public health research but also routine health surveillance and reporting (Wanless 2004). There are legal issues enshrined in the Data Protection Act 1998 (see Chapter 29 of the Act) that prevent sharing of personal information for research without prior consent. Section 60 of the Health and Social Care Act 2001 (see Chapter 15 of the Act) attempted to provide a legal basis for public health research, but the mechanism is slow and difficult to satisfy. In addition, guidance aimed at preventing inadvertent disclosure does not flow directly from the legislation and causes particular problems for small populations, relatively rare events, areas where administrative boundaries do not match, and marginal geographic changes. The sharing of data and information between NHS organizations is proving problematic. It was hoped that the public health strategy, *Choosing health,* would address this threat to public health surveillance and public health research. A balance between individual confidentiality and public health requirements must be found.

The Office for National Statistics ran a consultation between February and April 2006 on guidance on disclosure issues that arise when handling health statistics (Office for National Statistics 2006).

CONCLUSIONS

There can be little doubt that there is a growing level of interest in making better use of information to improve health. The entry into the information arena of a growing number of private organizations underlines this point. In the next few years we are likely to see more of these and possibly a further development of public–private partnerships in this field. The decision by the NHS Health and Social Care Information Centre to create a new company with Dr Foster (a private sector company dealing with health information) is a clear signal of the direction of travel. Such developments are to be welcomed if they allow the skills of the private sector – particularly those involving communication and dissemination – to be combined with the expertise in the NHS and academic departments.

126

There is still considerable work to do in addressing the currently confusing guidance on information governance, and a sensible balance has to found between the possible risks of disclosure and the public good delivered by public sector bodies.

Technological developments are increasingly likely to continue – an online world will mean that people (both professionals and private individuals) will demand instant access to information about health and health services.

In short, we are all striving towards a vision of better data, better information, better health.

DISCUSSION QUESTIONS

1   Are the data sources and types available to public health sufficient to measure health need?

2   Are there deficits or gaps in the data and, if so, how might these be filled?

3   Why is so little use often made of the data and information that exist?

4   With more diversity evident in the production of health information, what opportunities and threats does this pose?

REFERENCES

Association of Public Health Observatories (2005) *Sources of data on lifestyle risk factors in local populations.* Technical Briefing No. 1. London: APHO.

Association of Public Health Observatories (2006) *Collection of reports on indications of public health in the English regions.* London: APHO. Available from URL: <http://www.apho.org.uk/apho/viewResource.aspx?id=2679>.

Carr-Hill, R. and Chalmers-Dixon, P. (2005) *The public health observatory handbook of health inequalities measurement.* London: South East Public Health Observatory.

Census Act 1920. Chapter 41. London: HMSO.

Data Protection Act 1998. Chapter 29. London: HMSO.

Department of Health (2006a) *Informing healthier choices: information and intelligence for health populations.* London: Department of Health.

Department of Health (2006b) *Measuring childhood obesity: guidance to PCTs on data handling.* London: Department of Health.

Donaldson, L.J. and Donaldson, R.J. (2003) *Essential public health,* 2nd edition (revised). London: Petroc Press.

European Union (1997) *Treaty of Amsterdam: amending the Treaty on European Union, the treaties establishing the European communities and related acts. Official Journal C 340.*

European Union (2004) *Eurostat: your key to European statistics.* Brussels: European Union. Available from: URL: <http://epp.ekurostat.cec.eu.int/>.

Gnani, S. and Majeed, A. (2006) *A user's guide to data collected in primary care in England.* London: Association of Public Health Observatories.

Health and Social Care Act 2001. Chapter 15. London: HMSO.

Healthcare Commission (2006) *The 'better metrics' project.* Version 7. London: Healthcare Commission. Available from URL: <http://www.osha.nhs.uk/>.

Hemmings, J. and Wilkinson, J.R. (2003) What is a public health observatory? *Journal of Epidemiology and Community Health,* 57: 324–326.

HM Treasury (1999) *Building trust in statistics.* Cm 4412. London: HM Treasury.

NHS Modernization Agency (2002) *Coronary heart disease. Collaborative service improvement guide: secondary prevention.* London: NHS Modernization Agency.

Office of the Deputy Prime Minister (2004) *Index of multiple deprivation 2004 (IMD2004).* London: ODPM.

Office for National Statistics (2002) *Code of practice: statement of principles.* London: HMSO.

Office for National Statistics (2003) *Discussion Paper: Proposals for an Integrated Population Statistics System.* London: ONS.

Office for National Statistics (2006) *Review of the dissemination of health statistics consultation document.* London: ONS.

Secretary of State for Health (1999) *Saving lives: our healthier nation.* Cm 4386. London: HMSO.

Secretary of State for Health (2004) *Choosing health – making healthier choices easier.* Cm 6374. London: HMSO.

Secretary of State for Health (2006) *Our health, our care, our say: a new direction for community services.* Cm 6737. London: HMSO.

Transport and Health Study Group (2003) *Carrying out a health impact assessment of a transport policy.* London: Faculty of Public Health Medicine.

University of Essex (2006) *UK Data Archive (UKDA).* Available from: <http://www.date-archive.ac.uk/>.

Wanless, D. (2002) *Securing our future health: taking a long term view.* Final report. London: HM Treasury.

Wanless, D. (2004) *Securing good health of the whole population.* Final report. London: HM Treasury.

Chapter 6

Research-informed public health

John Øvretveit

KEY POINTS OF THIS CHAPTER

- Evidence-based public health is neither desirable nor feasible
- Considerable benefits can be derived from a more research-informed public health
- Research can help to inform public health management decisions
- Changes that need to be made to lead to a more research-informed public health

INTRODUCTION

The purpose of this chapter is not to present the evidence that public health programmes are effective; rather, it is to describe how research can help to inform public health management decisions and to consider how a more research-informed public health can be developed. It describes examples of research that public health managers have used, discusses research methods, and considers practical changes that need to be made. The chapter is intended for public health managers, managers of health care services, and health researchers. It discusses the relationships between these parties and how research is initiated, conducted and used. Some questions addressed include:

- What type of evidence is needed by managers to decide whether and how to improve public health?
- Is this evidence available or can it be produced?
- What are the challenges in developing the evidence base for public health?

129

■ What can managers and researchers do to make more use of research to improve public health?

The theme of the chapter is that an evidence-based public health is neither desirable nor feasible, but there are great benefits to a more research-informed public health. Both public health managers and researchers have a part to play in achieving this. The first part of the chapter presents examples of the use of evidence in public health management. These examples raise issues about the type of evidence that is useful to public health managers and about the methods for generating this evidence. Part two asks whether an evidence-based public health is desirable and possible. It considers the debate about appropriate research methods and alternative approaches. The third part of the chapter discusses changes that can lead to a more research-informed public health.

EXAMPLES OF THE USE OF EVIDENCE IN PUBLIC HEALTH MANAGEMENT

Epidemiology

An early comparative study found Finland to have the highest rates of heart disease in the seven countries studied. This provided the impetus for action, and community-based health promotion programmes were developed based on experience with similar programmes. The long-term evaluation of these programmes showed them to be successful, but also the challenges in showing a reduction in mortality and even changes in behaviour were due to the programme and not to other changes. The evidence, although controversial, has been used to improve the programme and establish many others (Jousilahti *et al.* 1995; Puska *et al.* 1989).

Smoking cessation

The time to create credible evidence in public health and the challenges in doing so are demonstrated in the example of the harmful effects of smoking on health. It is also an example of both the power and limits of evidence alone to effect change in policy. A faster application of research into practice can be seen in the use of evidence about effective ways to stop smoking. Research has used theories about habit change and evaluation to design and discover which approaches are effective.

Policy-makers in Stockholm, Sweden, were influenced by research showing that only 7 per cent of smokers trying to stop were successful at 12 months (Zhu *et al.* 2000), and that this rate could be increased by help from physicians and/or specialist cessation counsellors. Local research also showed a shortage of cessation counsellors, but also that telephone support services could increase the 12-month cessation rate to 30 per cent (Helgason *et al.* 2004). The city established a professionally run stop-smoking telephone line, which was a great success. Research into users of this service found that more were able to stop when they used nicotine replacement therapy, additional support from a health professional, and were not exposed to second-hand smoke, than were able to when they received a proactive rather than a reactive telephone service. The research led to improvements to the service that have increased 12-month quit rates.

Challenges for evaluative research into public health programmes

The 'Heartbeat Wales' programme in the UK for changing behaviours that increased the risk of cardiovascular disease was based on research into community programmes in Finland and the USA (Jousilahti *et al.* 1995). It included a TV programme, and projects for smoking cessation, nutrition, restaurants, and workplace programmes (Tudor-Smith *et al.* 1998). An evaluation of five-year effects found some behavioural changes such as better diet and reduced smoking in those surveyed. However, it was not possible to tell from the research whether the programme was effective, and the study was of limited value for practical public health decision-making. The reasons are well summarized by the researchers:

> The major conclusion to be drawn from this study is that the basic quasi experimental design was inappropriate and insufficiently sensitive to answer the complex research questions being asked. By their very nature, successful long term community based programmes can result in complex and wide ranging effects, many of which may be unexpected and not confined to one predetermined intervention community, making the measurement of any impact and attribution of causality highly problematic. Solving these problems will remain a continuing dilemma for advocates of prevention and should be a cause for reflection among academics and researchers concerning appropriate methods for assessing the results from such programmes. New evaluation techniques need to be developed that combine the strengths of quantitative and qualitative research methods and make better use of more proximal outcomes.
>
> (Tudor-Smith *et al.* 1998)

EVIDENCE-BASED PUBLIC HEALTH?

Evidence-based medicine is a clinician deciding with a patient the best action, by using the latest research evidence, usually about treatment effectiveness, combined with the clinician's experience. Clinical professions have always used both the scientific base of the profession and personal clinical experience to guide their practice. As more and better research became available, and the profession's authority declined, a movement developed to make greater use of this research in clinical decisions.

The impact of this movement on clinical practice is sometimes exaggerated, but there are more pressures on clinicians to use research and justify their decisions in relation to recent research. At other levels, policy and guidance affecting clinical decisions is becoming more evidence based: professional specialities provide clinical guidelines based on reviews of evidence, and national health technology assessment bodies issue authoritative guidance that is increasingly difficult for providers to ignore.

The concepts of evidence-based health care management (Walshe and Rundall 2001), policy (Cochrane 1972; Ham et al. 2005) and public health (Kirkwood 2004) have also been advanced. However, these concepts have had less impact on practice and on research in these fields. The amount and quality of research is less, the certainty about effectiveness provided by the research is lower, and the way in which research can and should influence decision-making is more complex and different to how clinical decisions are made about individual patients.

The debate

Why is public health less evidence based than clinical medicine, as Derek Wanless in the UK and others have alleged (Wanless 2004)? First there are those who would disagree that it is, citing the gap between clinicians' practice and latest research, and also citing a number of public health interventions for which there is good evidence (Kelly 2004). Second, evidence about health needs and inequalities in a number of countries is relatively good – it is, rather, evidence about intervention effectiveness, especially the larger complex social programmes and policies, that is lacking in comparison to clinical medicine.

Part of the debate arises because, as earlier chapters have shown, 'public health' covers a broad range of 'interventions' or actions: from secondary prevention such as cancer screening, through primary prevention such as vaccination, to complex intersectoral programmes to reduce health inequalities, or health promotion programmes such as healthy eating. Within health promotion itself there is a wide range of actions, as Speller et al. (1997), in discussing the search for evidence of effective health promotion, noted: from awareness raising campaigns, information and advice, influencing policy, lobbying for change, training personnel, to community development, and sometimes all of these in combination.

The range is from individual, clinical-based public health actions, such as prescribing nicotine patches, to population programmes such as HIV/AIDS prevention publicity. Some are easier to evaluate than others, and it is likely that different evaluation methods would be needed for different types of intervention in different circumstances (Øvretveit 1998).

132

There tends to be more evidence for the effectiveness of individual clinical-based actions than for population health promotion. The effects of the latter on health and illness are more difficult to detect because the programmes may not be fully implemented, and because of the longer time taken before effects could be expected to show and of the influence of other factors such as changes in employment, income or housing.

Part of the debate relates to how much evidence should be used to decide the balance of resources between public health, on the one hand, and health care and acute medicine on the other. More of the public want public health and health promotion programmes, but not at the cost of less health care. Given a choice, politicians and the public will put responsive emergency medical care and acute care before health promotion, even if the evidence is clear that health promotion would reduce the need for some acute care. This debate relates to how much government and public services should promote a long-term approach, and increasingly the pressure is to be less 'paternalistic' and more short term and reactive. To what extent should evidence of effectiveness determine public health actions, especially when governments, as in the UK, are fearful of being labelled 'the nanny state' and are emphasizing the importance of personal choice (Jochelson 2005; Hunter 2005)?

A historical perspective

Increased attention to 'evidence-based public health', however, is not just a response to external developments: public health has long been concerned with developing methods to evaluate the effectiveness of interventions and to improve implementation using this evidence. Systematic studies into the determinants of ill health and risk factors have been accompanied by the application of similar methods to study interventions. The famous early practitioner of public health who provided evidence of contaminated water at a London public water source also used similar systematic methods to show the results of the intervention he made – data that were necessary to sustain the intervention and spread similar changes elsewhere after public complaints about the changes to the water supply.

With the development of the randomized controlled trial (RCT) in clinical medicine came a recognition of the value of this method and its more widespread use in clinical research. Public health researchers began to apply the method to a number of public health interventions (Solberg et al. 2000). Both successes with and challenges to the use of RCTs led to debate within public health, and especially in health promotion, about the view that only evidence of effectiveness from RCTs could be considered valid evidence (Macdonald et al. 1996).

Other evaluation methods with a long history in public health were described as alternatives, especially in situations where an RCT appeared not to be possible for practical and ethical reasons (Oliver and Peersman 2001). Some researchers also proposed that other evaluation methods were more appropriate, and not only as a 'second best': other methods gave more information about how the intervention worked or failed to work – knowledge that was often absent in RCT studies, even when complemented by parallel process evaluations (Victora *et al.* 2004).

Along with these developments in public health research came a recognition by some funders and politicians that timely information about public health interventions was useful for decision-making. Information from traditional scientific research was sometimes not so useful, not only because it did not always address practical questions but also because the situation had often changed by the time the information became available.

There is currently debate about the feasibility and value about an evidence-based approach to public health along similar lines to the debate in clinical medicine. The danger of privileging only those public health interventions with 'proven effectiveness' would result in the exclusion of many existing interventions, including interventions with some benefits proven through types of research that has not used randomized or even controlled trials.

Paradigm wars

In research there are debates about what type of evidence is credible about effectiveness, and about the value of other types of evidence. In simple terms the positivist paradigm views credible evidence as that produced by research that treats a public health action as an experiment. This involves planning data gathering in advance of the action, using a comparison group to control for other explanations for outcomes, randomly allocating people or organizations to experimental and control groups to control for other influences, and measuring before and after characteristics of people using objective measures and quantitative data that can be analysed statistically.

It is often not possible to plan and do public health research in this way, but different quasi-experimental designs can be and have been used that do not require random allocation and that allow retrospective analysis. However, they aspire to the ideal RCT design and operate within the positivist paradigm.

A critique of this approach is that the older natural science concepts of causality are not appropriate in the social field and that effects cannot be clearly proven by evaluations (Guba and Lincoln 1989). Instead, a 'naturalistic' approach to evaluation was proposed, studying the intervention in its natural context and understanding stakeholders' perceptions of 'effects'.

Relatively early in the development of 'programme evaluation' in the USA, Weiss (1972) and Cronbach *et al.* (1980) emphasized the 'context-bound' nature of social programmes – they were constructed to answer specific problems in specific contexts, and evaluation should be 'contextually realistic'. Programmes 'unfold' in a unique way in relation to the context and the social questions addressed. This makes generalization difficult.

This approach was further elaborated by Guba and Lincoln's (1989) 'Fourth generation evaluation', which proposed that evaluations should concentrate on describing how a programme evolves in relation to its social context. More recently, these ideas have been developed in social research by Pawson and Tilley (1997) and in health care by Øvretveit (1998). This paradigm also takes a different view about the role of the evaluator as part of the social context, with the possibility of providing feedback during implementation in order to improve the programme (Øvretveit 2002).

Related to these ideas is the notion of 'programme theory', which is a theory of how the programme works to have its effects. The programme theory can be the one developed by the evaluators, or based on the implicit assumptions of the intervention actors about 'mechanisms and results'. 'Theory-driven evaluation' is where the evaluator derives a theory of what are the active components of a programme and the mechanisms by which they have immediate, intermediate and distal outcomes (Lipsey 1990; Chen and Rossi 1987; Chen 1990). This theory needs to be formulated to guide the evaluation data collection and then tested in the analysis. To some degree, Green and Kreuter's (1999) precede/proceed health promotion model uses this approach: in the precede part each of the educational, organizational, social, epidemiological, and environmental assessments corresponds to the other set of indicators of the proceed part about outcomes.

The paradigm difference

The main differences between the two paradigms are in the way each:

- deals with the conditions surrounding the intervention and how these influence the intervention or may change (e.g. media coverage of a health issue after a public programme has been introduced, wealth of the area in which people targeted by the intervention live);
- views the validity of subjective perceptions of involved or observing actors as evidence, both of outcome and of the degree of implementation of the public health programme.

The positivist experimental and constructivist paradigms agree about the influence of conditions surrounding an intervention, but disagree about how evaluation should deal with these influences. In the experimental paradigm the influences are regarded as confounders, and designs using controls and/or statistical analyses are used to exclude them when assessing the effects of an intervention. This abstracts the intervention from its surrounding conditions, making generalization possible, and implies that replicating the intervention in any conditions will produce similar results.

The constructivist or naturalistic paradigm views these conditions not as a set of confounders but as influences that can both help and hinder the action, and which need to be understood rather than 'controlled out'. This approach views a public health action as a unique and constantly changing event, interpreted differently by different 'actors'. Evidence about effectiveness of one intervention in one situation can only be gained by examining how the intervention and situation changed and the perceptions of stakeholders about the results. (Lincoln and Guba 1985; Guba and Lincoln 1989)). This paradigm also accepts other types of evidence as valid, including people perceptions of events and judgements of effectiveness.

What is 'valid evidence' for public health?

If useful 'evidence' is viewed solely as evidence about needs and effectiveness, or that which is generated by epidemiology or from randomized controlled trials, then public health will never be evidence based (see Box 6.1). However, if 'evidence' is defined more broadly then many public health actions are or could be 'evidence based'. A broader definition accepts the following as valid evidence for public health decision-making:

Intermediate outcomes of actions

- changes to people's attitudes, which are likely to affect their behaviour;
- changes to people's behaviour, which are likely to affect their health.

Perceptions about outcomes and choices

- the perception of professionals and other 'informed observers' about changes to patients or the public's attitudes, behaviours or health that they think were due to the public health action;
- public preferences about different actions and about choices between different ways to allocate resources.

Evidence about implementation

- data about the degree to which a planned public health action was implemented;
- data about conditions that helped and hindered implementation.

This broader definition of evidence and the naturalistic/constructivist paradigm is gaining ground in public health, which has tended to adopt uncritically the research methods of clinical medicine. There is more research into and evidence about health needs, inequalities, and clinical public health interventions than research into population interventions and about actions to reduce health inequalities. Public health managers need to know not only what the health problems and needs are and whether a type of action was effective, but why it was effective, as well as different stakeholders' perceptions. They need to know which conditions helped and hindered implementation in order to decide whether or how to carry out the action in their

---

BOX 6.1   CHALLENGES IN EVALUATING MANY PUBLIC HEALTH PROGRAMMES

Some of the challenges that, in most circumstances, prevent the use of clinical research evaluation designs with controls and statistical probability analyses include:

- randomization is often not possible;
- the intervention cannot be standardized or held constant – it is often a multiple component intervention carried out in different stages, at different levels and constantly evolving;
- control or even comparison groups are often difficult to arrange;
- the environment 'surrounding' the intervention is often changing, with confounding influences increasing and decreasing at different times;
- a range of short- and long-term outcome data need to be collected to study issues of concern to different stakeholders;
- some key expected health outcomes are often some time in the future – it is difficult to be sure that these outcomes are caused by the intervention and not by something else.

(Øvretveit 2004)

---

local situation. Managers and public health scientists alike want to know which aspects of more complex action-interventions were critical and how important it is to have a combination of actions working as an 'intervention system'. To generate this knowledge, a wider range of research methods than those traditionally used in public health are needed. The Word Health Organization Health Evidence Network defines evidence as 'findings from research and any other knowledge that could be useful in decision-making on public health and health care' (WHO HEN 2005).

Summary: research informed, not evidence based

Political and value choices will always be a key factor in public health decisions, and evidence of effectiveness will rarely be as certain as for some clinical treatments. Public health never will be, or should be, evidence based, but it needs to become more research informed (see Box 6.2). This means making better decisions by finding and using local and published research of many types into population health needs, people's perceptions, how programmes and policies are implemented, and effectiveness and costs. For this to happen, there will need to be changes to the amount and type of research undertaken, how it is made available to practitioners, and to managers' abilities to use a range of research. How can this be achieved?

137

BOX 6.2   DEFINITIONS

Research-informed public health
Making decisions about how to improve public health using research carried out elsewhere as well as local research. Research for better-informed decisions includes published and local epidemiological and demographic studies, research into effectiveness, cost effectiveness, implementation processes, and stakeholder perceptions.

Evaluation-informed public health
Evaluation-informed public health is an important part of a research-informed approach to public health action. It is making management and policy decisions by using research from elsewhere, using local evidence about implementation, effectiveness and costs, and using evaluation concepts to plan actions.

TOWARDS A MORE RESEARCH-INFORMED PUBLIC HEALTH

There is a strong argument for making more use of research in decisions about public health, both in setting the agenda and in making better-informed decisions. For this to happen changes will be needed to research and to management practice and education. This section of the chapter first considers methodological challenges and ways forward for generating the range of evidence that public health managers require. It then describes changes needed in the research process of initiating, commissioning, designing, and conducting research to make it more useful and accessible to managers. The third section discusses how research and management education, capacity and practice can be developed for a more research-informed public health.

Research design and methods

Epidemiological and experimental methods will continue to be a key source of evidence for public health management. More sophisticated statistical analysis and database linking are just two developments to methods in this field. One example is a study estimating smoking prevalence in each local primary trust area in England, generated by linking mortality data and information from household surveys and using synthetic estimation analysis (Twigg *et al.* 2004).

138

In addition, developments are also taking place in methods for understanding whether and how some of the more complex public health actions work. This involves researchers using a wider range of methods, as well as public health managers carrying out local feedback evaluation studies to inform their decisions. In some cases local feedback studies may meet scientific standards for publication. The following considers non-traditional methods that can generate useful evidence for public health managers.

The constructivist and naturalistic critique of positivist research methods was outlined above. To produce more useful evidence, future research and methods development can take place in two areas: adding qualitative data to traditional statistical experimental designs, and in developing methods to better understand which conditions help and hinder public health interventions and how they do so.

Experimental designs can be developed by making more use of inter-mediate outcome indicators. They can also include stakeholders' perceptions about implementation and outcomes and incorporate these qualitative data into the study. Table 6.1 shows the range of types of evidence that are needed and which can be generated with this combined approach.

Understanding critical conditions

Other methods and designs need to be developed to produce knowledge about which results are achieved, by which types of actions, in which situations, and how these results were achieved. The critique of experimental designs is not just that the

Table 6.1 *Range and types of evidence*

	Description of degree of implementation	Description of **results** (Outcome measures, and extent to which the intervention influenced these results)	Description of **conditions** (Other factors that influenced results and that helped and hindered the intervention implementation)
Types of evidence			
Experiential evidence	A: Informants reports	B: Informants reports	C: Informants theories
Statistical/ quantitative evidence	D: Monitoring indicators	E: Probability that Y outcomes were caused by X intervention	F: Conclusions from statistical analysis controlling for different confounder

methods are often difficult to apply to changing complex public health actions. Perhaps more important is the 'black box' critique – that if an experimental study does show that an intervention produced certain outcomes, it does not help us understand how the intervention worked, and which components and which conditions were critical for the results. The assumption is that reproducing the intervention will produce the same results elsewhere. The naturalist critique is that complex interventions cannot and should not be reproduced like a standard treatment, but have to be tailored to the local situation: that these actions are unique and depend on certain 'surrounding' conditions to have their effects.

One question that follows is that if the findings cannot be generalized, what is the value to managers of knowing this? The answer is that it is better for managers not to assume that they can reproduce the intervention and its conditions. Rather, by knowing the details of implementation and which conditions were critical, they are better able to make the translation to their setting and plan and carry out an action that is likely to be implemented and to be effective.

A second question is which methods to use to understand how the action has its effects in specific circumstances and to identify which conditions are critical. Methods can be classified into two broad approaches. The 'subjective' approach collects and analyses a range of observing or involved informants' theories about which parts of the programme have the largest effect and which conditions helped and hindered both implementation and the effects. The second is the 'objective' approach, which seeks to identify the critical elements and factors that informants may not be conscious of and without reference to them. This usually involves designs that compare programme areas with those without the programme and investigates the presence and absence of factors theorized by the researchers to be critical. A combined approach can also be used.

Local feedback evaluation

A more research-informed public health also means public health managers getting and using data about local health problems and programmes. As regards programme evaluation, designs and methods do not have to be as expensive or rigorous as would be required for scientific publication. The aim is to gather data to help improve the programme and accountability, not to investigate to a high degree of certainty that the programme is effective, especially if the programme design is based on research indicating that it is effective elsewhere. Currently, public health managers have little reliable data to assess their programme implementation and intermediate results, and the aim is to improve on this rather than meet rigorous scientific standards. However, minimum research standards are required so that the findings are not misleading. A variety of action evaluation and process evaluation methods can give improvement and accountability feedback, and sometimes reach sufficient standards for publishing (Fawcett *et al.* 1997; Greene 1993; Øvretveit 2002).

THE COMMISSIONING AND CONDUCT OF PUBLIC HEALTH RESEARCH

A wider range of research methods and evidence will be more helpful to public health managers, but changes are also required in how research is commissioned, conducted and made available. Managers and policy-makers will need to be more involved in the research process, but there also need to be safeguards to prevent overly political-directed research or fashionable topics driving out long-term research. There is a tension between the academic interests of researchers to study certain topics in certain ways, and the needs of managers for timely information at a low cost, which often means of a lower scientific quality. Greater willingness of journals to publish 'practical research' may reduce this tension, but it can also result in research that is misleading because studies have not observed basic scientific standards or described the limitations.

Identifying research subjects and questions

Traditionally public health research questions have been identified by reference to previous research and theory. This is not to say that research has not addressed practical questions or formulated implications for action, but that the primary driver is public health science rather than contemporary practical issues. Public health managers and policy-makers will play a greater role in deciding which subjects and questions are studied, but need to do so with an understanding of public health research. Two examples of good practice in combining the scientific and the practice are the reviews of evidence commissioned by the former English Health Development Agency (HDA) and the English NHS Service Development and Organization (SDO) R&D Programme. Research consumers are surveyed for subjects about which they require research evidence, and researchers are commissioned to review the evidence on these subjects. HDA has mapped out 'what we know' and 'need to know' in a number of areas. These surveys of research consumers' needs and reviews of evidence allow those commissioning research to give researchers specific guidance for their proposals and allow better assessments of proposals.

Changes are also taking place in non-governmental funding agencies, which are now giving a higher value to the practical value of research in their funding policy and guidance to research proposers. Scientific reviews of proposals are still a key part in funding decisions, but the likely practical value of the research is carrying a higher weight. An example concerns one Australian research commissioning process that requires researchers to estimate the 'pay-back value' of their research.

Making research accessible

There is a view that research methods or commissioning should not be changed, but rather that research should be made more accessible to public health managers.

Certainly there is much completed research that could be used by managers, but it is difficult for managers to find and assess the scientific quality and the practical implications.

Accessibility needs to improve, regardless of the above changes. This is needed in three areas: finding the research, report summaries, and syntheses of research:

■ *Finding the research*. Easier ways for managers to find published research and project reports are needed and have been developed. Electronic internet databases have been set up that give access to research, reports and summaries; good examples are the former UK Health Development Agency database of public health interventions (HDAHealthPromis) and the EPPI database of health promotion research reports (Bibliomap, DoPher and TRoPHI).

■ *Research report summaries*. Summaries of research reports are needed that state clearly the practical implications for managers and public health practitioners, the limitations of the evidence, and issues to address when translating the research to other settings. Traditionally, both published and unpublished reports have not summarized results for practical action. Structured abstracts requiring this are being used in the health management field. In addition, evaluation reports need to describe more clearly details of the intervention, the conditions under which it was carried out, and any changes during implementation, in order to allow managers to assess whether or how to translate to their local setting (Des Jarlais *et al.* 2004).

■ *Research syntheses*. These are summaries of all the research on subjects of interest to public health managers, which assess the scientific quality, synthesize the findings, and provide practical recommendations. In the last five years methods have been developed for these reviews and syntheses that are appropriate for public health, and are increasingly used. Examples are the reviews commissioned for public health policy-makers, questions by the WHO public health evidence network (WHO HEN 2005), and reviews by HDA and the EPPI groups noted above.

DEVELOPING RESEARCH CAPACITY AND PUBLIC HEALTH MANAGERS

Developing researchers and research capacity

The discussion earlier noted some of the new methods that hold promise for providing more useful evidence. University-based researchers and research units need to be strengthened to generate this evidence, especially in research skills using social science and action evaluation methods. Departments of public health also have a key role in carrying out traditional surveys and monitoring and evaluation studies for improving actions they are carrying out. Often small departmental size will mean linking closely with other departments to gain the skills or conduct the research.

CASE STUDY

Developing implementation and evaluation competence in a department of health promotion

Faced with increasing competition for funding from clinical departments, the Stockholm Department of Public Health carried out a review of its evaluation skills and activities. The review found a demand in the department for evidence to justify their proposals, a concern about lack of skills and time to evaluate projects, and an assumption that the only valid evaluation would be one using a sophisticated experimental design.

The department established a database of skills that allowed people quickly to draw on other colleagues with the required skills for projects and for internal education. It also set up a programme to develop skills in evidence-based implementation and in action evaluation.

Developing public health managers and their departments

New research methods and research commissioning and dissemination will provide more useful research. But public health managers will also need to become more research literate, and to develop certain skills if they are to make use of this resource. This includes skills to search for and assess both qualitative and quantitative studies for their scientific quality and transferability potential, skills to manage or commission local research, and skills to present evidence appropriately in reports, proposals or presentations.

Two specific areas to develop are to make more use of 'implementation theory', and quality assurance tools in planning. The health promotion literature especially is unanimous in emphasizing that the chances for effective health promotion will increase if there are systematic and planned undertakings. However, systematic planning and implementation does not mean an inflexible approach. Indeed, a systematic approach that requires regular reviews and corrections makes a flexible approach more likely: it ensures that changes in the situation are taken account of and corrections made. Nor does it mean that planning cannot be participatory and that planning is separate from and precedes carrying out a programme. There is a consensus that those whose cooperation will be needed to carry out the programme, or who are the beneficiaries, should be part of the planning process. Again, a systematic approach ensures that this is achieved, and it is notable that these principles are embodied in the quality-assurance frameworks for health promotion summarized later.

A number of texts emphasize the connection between implementation and evaluation, and some frameworks clearly link the two (e.g. NORAD 1999). If a programme is well planned then it is easy to evaluate it against the planned objectives and indicators. Indeed, indicators can be collected as part of implementation (monitoring) for project correction. The evaluator then collates the monitoring reports or data, in addition to collecting other data to complete the evaluation.

Some quality-assurance tools are based on research into effective public health actions. One example is the tool developed for quality assurance of health promotion by the Swedish association of local authorities (Berensson *et al.* 1996). This was tested in a number of circumstances, and also draws on research to develop quality indicators for health promotion (Ader *et al.* 2001). The guidelines are in the form of 42 questions to assessors and/or practitioners, which probe whether good practices derived from research are being followed in the

- *structure of the project*: goals, target group, model/plan, responsibility, organization, resources;
- *project process*: support/participation, network, reception;
- *results:* changes in behaviour, changes in morbidity and mortality, environmental operational and social changes, and sustainable improvements.

Summary

Changes are needed for a more research-informed public health. A wider range of methods need to be used, with more implementation research, more research into public perceptions, and more involvement of managers and consumers in different parts of the research process. For this to happen, researchers and managers need to gain new skills and the capacity of their departments must be strengthened.

CONCLUSIONS

It is difficult to evaluate whether many public health actions are effective, but this does not mean they are not effective. There are more pressures to justify public health actions by reference to evidence of effectiveness, both elsewhere and in relation to local projects. More and better research is needed, and new methods hold promise for reducing at least some of the evidence gap between public health and clinical medicine. Public health managers need to use this research, develop skills to translate the research to their local setting, and make more use of existing data and small-scale local research to make their programmes more effective. One aspect of developing public health management is to provide accessible relevant research and to strengthen the capability of managers to apply and lead research. More research into programme implementation and results in different situations is needed, using different designs, at a national and at a local level, to provide feedback for programme improvement and accountability.

DISCUSSION QUESTIONS

1   Are there any public health actions for which there is conclusive evidence of effectiveness?
2   What are the challenges in evaluating the effectiveness of health promotion programmes such as exercise or healthy eating programmes?
3   How can public health research be made more useful to public health and health care managers?
4   How can public health management be developed to make more use of research?
5   Would public health projects and programmes receive significantly more funding and support if there was more credible evidence of effectiveness or cost-effectiveness?
6   Should limited finance for research be used for more rigorous randomized controlled trials, or for more process evaluations of how the programme was implemented and participants' perceptions of effectiveness?
7   Are combined RCT and process evaluations of value? If so, why?

REFERENCES

Ader, M., Berensson, K., Carlsson, P., Granath, M. and Urwitz, V. (2001) Quality indicators for health promotion programmes. *Health Promotion International*, 16(2): 187–195.

Berensson, K., Granath, M., Urwitz, V. and Bjorklund, E. (1996) *Succeeding with health promotion projects*, Stockholm: Lanstingsforbundet (http//:www.skl.se).

Chen, H. (1990) *Theory-Driven Evaluation*. London: Sage.

Chen, H. and Rossi, P. (1987) The theory driven approach to validity. *Evaluation and Program Planning*, 10: 95–103.

Cochrane, A. (1972) *Effectiveness and Efficiency*. London: Nuffield Provincial Hospitals Trust.

Cronbach, I., Ambron, S., Dornbush, S., Hess, R., Hornik, R., Phillips, D., Walker, D. and Weiner, S. (1980) *Towards reform in programme evaluation*. San Francisco: Jossey-Bass.

Des Jarlais, D.C., Lyes, C., Crepaz, N., and the TREND Group (2004) Improving the reporting – quality of nonrandomized evaluations: the TREND statement. *American Journal of Public Health*, 94: 361–366.

145

Fawcett, J. *et al.* (1997) in I. Rootman and D. McQueen (eds) *Evaluating health promotion approaches*. Copenhagen: WHO.

Green, L. and Kreuter, M. (1999) *Health promotion planning. An educational and environmental approach,* 2nd edition. Mountain View: Mayfield.

Greene, J. (1993) Qualitative program evaluation, in N. Denzin and Y. Lincoln (eds) *Handbook of qualitative research*. London: Sage, pp. 530–544.

Guba, E. and Lincoln, Y. (1989) *Fourth generation evaluation,* London: Sage.

Ham, C., Hunter, D. and Robinson, R. (1995) Evidence based policymaking. *British Medical Journal,* 310: 71–72.

Health Development Agency database of evidence briefings: httl1://www.hda.nhs.uk/html/research/evidencebase.html (accessed 13 May 2005).

Helgason, A., Tomson, T., Lund, K., Galanti, R., Ahnve, S. and Gilljam, H. (2004) Factors related to abstinence in a telephone helpline for smoking cessation. *European Journal of Public Health,* 14: 1–5.

Hunter, D.J. (2005) Choosing or losing health? *Journal of Epidemiology & Community Health,* 59(12): 1010–1013.

Jochelson, K. (2005) *Nanny or steward? The role of government in public health.* London: King's Fund.

Jousilahti, P., Korhonen, H.J., Vartiainen, E. and Puska, P. (1995) The community approach in the prevention of cardiovascular disease: evaluation of the Finnish experience in North Karelia (1972–1992). *Union Medicine Canada,* 124(2): 7–16.

Kelly, M. (2004) *The evidence of effectiveness of public health interventions – and the implications.* London: Health Development Agency.

Kirkwood, B. (2004) Making public health interventions more evidence based. *British Medical Journal,* 328: 966–967.

Lincoln, Y. and Guba, E. (1985) *Naturalistic Inquiry.* Newbury Park: Sage Publications.

Lipsey, M. (1990) Theories as methods: small theories of treatment, in L. Seechrest, E. Perrin and J. Bunker (eds) *Research methodology: strengthening causal interpretation of non-experimental data.* Washington, DC: US Department of Health and Human Services, pp. 33–51.

Macdonald, G., Veen, C. and Tones, K. (1996) Evidence for success in health promotion: suggestions for improvement. *Health Education Research,* 11(3): 367–376.

NORAD (1999) *The logical framework approach (LFA) for objectives oriented planning.* Oslo: Norwegian Agency for Development Cooperation.

Oliver, S. and Peersman, G. (eds) (2001) *Using research for effective health promotion.* Milton Keynes: Open University Press.

Øvretveit, J. (1998) *Evaluating health interventions.* Milton Keynes: Open University Press.

Øvretveit, J. (2002) *Action evaluation of health programmes and change. A handbook for a user focused approach.* Oxford: Radcliffe Medical Press.

Øvretveit, J. (2004) Evaluating complex social interventions. *Eurohealth*, 21–24.

Pawson, R. and Tilley, N. (1997) *Realistic evaluation*. London: Sage.

Puska, P., Tuomilehto, J., Nissinen, A., Salonen, J.T., Vartiainen, E., Pietinen, P., Koskela, K. and Korhonen, H.J. (1989) The North Karelia project: 15 years of community-based prevention of coronary heart disease. *Annals of Medicine*, 21(3): 169–173.

Solberg, L.I., Kottke, T.E., Brekke, M.L., Magnan, S., Davidson, G., Calomeni, C.A., Conn, S.A., Amundson, G.M. and Nelson, A. (2000) Failure of a continuous quality improvement intervention to increase the delivery of preventive services. A randomized trial. *Joint Commission Journal on Quality Improvement*, 26(9): 525–537.

Speller, V., Evans, D. and Head, M. (1997) Developing quality assurance standards for health promotion practice in the UK. *Health Promotion International*, 12: 215–224.

Tudor-Smith, C., Nutbeam, D., Moore, L. and Catford, J. (1998) Effects of the Heartbeat Wales programme over five years on behavioural risks for cardiovascular disease. *British Medical Journal*, 316: 818–822.

Twigg, L., Moon, G. and Walker, S. (2004) *The smoking epidemic in England*. London: Health Development Agency (www.had.nhs.uk).

Victora, C., Habicht, J. and Bryce, J. (2004) Evidence-based public health: moving beyond randomized trials. *American Journal of Public Health*, 94(3): 400–410.

Walshe, K. and Rundall, T. (2001) Evidence-based management: from theory to practice in health care. *The Milbank Quarterly*, 79(3): 429–457.

Wanless, D. (2004) *Securing good health for the whole population*. London: HM Treasury.

Weiss, C. (1972) Evaluating education and social action programmes, in C. Weiss (ed.) *Evaluating action programmes: readings in social action and education*. Boston: Allyn and Bacon, pp. 3–27.

WHO HEN (2005) World Health Organization Evidence Network database of reviews for policy-makers questions: http://www.euro.who.int/HEN (accessed 15 May 2005).

Zhu, S., Melcer, T., Sun, J., Rosbrook, B. and Pierce, M. (2000) Smoking cessation with and without assitance: a population based analysis. *American Journal of Preventive Medicine*, 18(4): 305–311.

Chapter 7

Developing leadership and management for health

Catherine Hannaway, Paul Plsek and David J. Hunter

KEY POINTS OF THIS CHAPTER

- Rehearses key meanings of public health management
- Identifies the core elements of managing for health
- Identifies training needs for the public health manager
- Presents a case study describing a leadership for health improvement programme that seeks to bring together many of the themes explored in earlier chapters
- Leadership for health improvement comprises three domains: leadership, improvement knowledge and skills, health improvement systems

---

INTRODUCTION

As earlier chapters have shown, the delivery of effective public health services requires a skilled competent workforce, often working in partnership and with the community. The public health challenges in today's complex and interdependent societies, which were reviewed in Chapter 1, cannot be met without an effective public health infrastructure. Few countries, however, either have the necessary policies and resources in place to ensure effective operation of the public health function at national and subnational levels, or are prepared to equip public health practitioners with the requisite skills to exploit fully their potential to improve the public's health. The notion of public health management (PHM) has been advanced as one means by which these problems and deficits may be addressed. It is not a panacea for the weaknesses and deficiencies that have been identified, although it does recognize the importance of a public health workforce that is equipped with the requisite skills for the tasks with which it has to deal. At the heart of PHM is a commitment to action and implementation.

Recalling the discussion in Chapter 3, public health management (PHM) is about

- mobilizing resources;
- managing the health and disease of a population;
- managing for population health.

PHM may be applied to a range of health systems. In developing competence in PHM, several questions arise:

- Who is PHM for?
- What are their needs and those of their employers?
- What should be the objectives of a PHM education/development programme?
- What should it cover in terms of content?
- Which learning methods should be included?
- Who should provide this education/development?
- Who should pay for it?
- How should PHM programmes be developed?

Various surveys and gaps/needs analyses have sought to identify the skills required for effective PHM. Inevitably, and rightly, different issues will arise in different countries concerning the development of capacity in PHM and the requisite training and development opportunities. For example, the WHO Regional Committee for Europe has proposed a list of key areas of competencies for public health (WHO 1999):

- understanding health and disease, assessing health status;
- evidence-based decisions, research and information management;
- disease surveillance and control;
- promoting health and well-being;
- evaluating and improving health outcomes and the effectiveness and efficiency of health care;
- management and leadership;
- intersectoral and collaborative working and coordination;
- advocacy and communication.

PHM courses are not plentiful. It is not simply a matter of looking just at formal Masters programmes, although there remains a need for these and for new and innovative ones; also to be considered are short courses, continuing professional development, distance learning, and e-learning.

The content of training for PHM might include some or all of the following topics:

- health needs assessment;
- prevention – primary and secondary;
- use of behavioural change theories;
- networks and alliance building;
- strategic management and planning;
- alternative budgeting systems;
- development of performance indicators;
- business planning;
- managing and leading health projects;
- management in complex adaptive systems marked by intersectoral settings;
- communication;
- creating and enhancing policy networks;
- power and politics;
- local strategy development;
- policy development;
- evaluation of clinical services;
- health services research.

This list emerges as critical for public health education and development. A significant part of the public health function demands coping with, and managing, change. This in turn requires committed leadership. Leadership, as was suggested in Chapter 1, complements management rather than being something entirely separate from it. As earlier chapters have demonstrated, for the most part public health leadership in the UK and elsewhere remains underdeveloped, both in respect of transformational and transactional leadership development. Both styles of leadership are required to bring about the scale of change needed to improve the public's health and to tackle health inequalities. They are required not only in health care services but in all those organizations engaged in health improvement.

As Nutbeam and Wise (2002) argue, public health intervention requires special skills that are different from the analytical skills required to assess health problems in a population.

> Influencing health behaviour in populations, and influencing the structural and environmental determinants of health, requires public health specialists to have substantial knowledge and skills in the behavioural, social, and political sciences.
>
> (Nutbeam and Wise 2002: 1883)

The stress on intervention also highlights the need for a different style of leadership:

> Leadership for public health intervention requires practitioners to work more closely with other sectors, to advocate effectively for the development and adoption of healthy public policy, and to create, with communities, a shared vision for the public's health.
>
> (Nutbeam and Wise 2002: 1883)

There are few programmes that explicitly address the need for advanced training for public health leadership. In England, the Department of Health has supported two distinctly different approaches to public health leadership development (Rao 2006). The first is the National Public Health Leadership Programme, which aims to develop the capabilities of individuals as leaders. The programme is multi-disciplinary and multisectoral and has 90 places distributed across three centres. It is open to participants from across the UK and from organizations such as the Armed Forces.

A recent independent evaluation of the impact of the programmes on public health delivery has demonstrated that the programme has not only benefited participants (personal effectiveness being the programme's principal purpose) but that health improvement has also been positively influenced as a result of behaviour change among participants.

The second approach supported by the Department of Health is the one-year Leadership for Health Improvement Programme (LHIP). The LHIP focuses both on individual leaders and on a more collaborative 'whole systems approach'. The one-year programme is currently confined to Yorkshire and Humber, and the North East regions and is supporting a cohort of around sixty local public health leaders from the NHS, local government, and related services such as the police and fire to create a network of individuals skilled in the areas of 'improvement knowledge and skills', 'leadership' and 'health improvement systems'. The central interest lies in the overlap between these three domains and in the synergy between them. Successful local delivery of health improvement will require leadership that will facilitate:

- building whole system relationships;
- understanding and using improvement methods;
- the development of exceptional leadership skills to move these areas forward.

The programme is being evaluated by a team from Northumbria University.

The LHIP's distinctiveness lies in seeking to apply improvement principles and tools to public health. Whereas hitherto improvement thinking has been applied with considerable success to health care services which resemble a closed, bounded system, its application to public health demands acknowledging that it is a very different system – open, porous and with no clear boundaries. In short, there is no improvement thinking script for public health – the LHIP participants and faculty will write it together. But there are some building blocks around to make a start.

151

BOX 7.1 TEN HIGH-IMPACT CHANGES FOR SERVICE IMPROVEMENT

- Treat day surgery (rather than inpatient surgery) as the norm for elective surgery.
- Improve patient flow across the whole NHS system by improving access to key diagnostic tests.
- Manage variation in patient discharge, thereby reducing length of stay.
- Manage variation in the patient admission process.
- Avoid unnecessary follow-ups for patients and provide necessary follow-ups in the right care setting.
- Increase the reliability of performing therapeutic interventions through a care bundle package.
- Apply a systematic approach to care for people with long-term conditions.
- Improve patient access by reducing the number of queues.
- Optimize patient flow through service bottlenecks using process templates.
- Redesign extended roles in line with efficient pathways to attract and retain an effective workforce.

For example, there are the ten High-Impact Changes for Service Improvement Delivery (NHS Modernization Agency 2004), listed in Box 7.1. Although these have been applied to acute services only, there is what might be described as a hierarchy of transferability. Some examples – notably improvement of flow, application of systematic approaches, improved access, and role redesign – have a clear applicability to the public health context.

This chapter describes the experience of LHIP as a case study of the type of development programme required to strengthen leadership and management for health improvement against a context of major changes in the way in which public services, including health, are being organized.

CASE STUDY

The Leadership for Health Improvement Programme (LHIP)

As a national pilot site, the NHS Yorkshire and Humber (formerly North and East Yorkshire and Northern Lincolnshire Strategic Health Authority) is running a one-year development programme for those who play key leadership roles in support of local health improvement across Yorkshire and the Humber and the North East of England. The LHIP seeks to develop individuals who excel at the intersection of three knowledge domains: leadership, improvement knowledge and skills, and health improvement systems (see Figure 7.1).

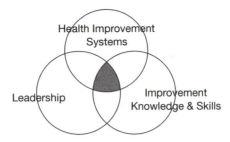

Figure 7.1 *The Leadership for Health Improvement Programme*

The framework builds on research previously undertaken for the NHS Leading Modernization Programme to define the knowledge, skills and capabilities that participants must have in these three areas in order to be successful. This research includes:

■ review of published work;
■ interviews with experts;
■ analysis of content of similar programmes;
■ discussions with participants;
■ integrating the Faculty of Public Health's 10 Competencies (in the process of being updated).

The findings are captured here as a framework for the LHIP. It is important to note that the items listed are in no particular order of priority. In creating the LHIP it was considered important that individuals decide for themselves the priority order that the knowledge, skills and, in some instances, behaviours, are most applicable to them in their own role.

High-level definitions and structure of the thinking

The three overlapping circles in Figure 7.1 represent the *knowledge domains* of interest in the scope of the LHIP. Brief, practical definitions of these three domains, in terms of what we are seeking to communicate to participants, are:

■ *Leadership:* the art of getting things done by enabling others to do more than they could or would do otherwise.
■ *Improvement knowledge and skills:* the study and practice of enhancing the performance of processes and systems of work.
■ *Health improvement systems:* the practical realities and future possibilities of how interconnected health improvement is experienced by staff, individuals and communities.

It is the area of overlap between these circles that primarily describes the core nature and purpose of the programme; that is, participants on the LHIP should be skilled in:

- leadership of improvement;
- improvement of public health systems;
- improvement of leadership.

The aim is to develop participants to function within the middle overlap of all three circles to achieve the LHIP vision of 'Exceptional Leadership for Health Improvement'. This constitutes the 'added value' of the LHIP.

While the LHIP framework described here lists skills associated with each domain, our principal interest lies in the synergy between the domains and in the centre where participants learn to use all these skills in concert as they lead health improvement efforts in their respective organizations and across their entire local health communities.

Domain: Leadership refers to the body of knowledge about engaging, inspiring, influencing, developing and enabling others towards the achievement of an overall goal or vision of the future.

How does the domain of leadership – *the art of getting things done by enabling others to do more than they could or would do otherwise* – inform efforts in the LHIP to develop exceptional leaders of health improvement?

Brief synopsis of the research findings
The main model espoused in the current leadership literature is that of Transformational Leadership **(TL)**. This model grew out of large research projects done mainly in the USA with subjects in general industry and the military. More recently a related, but not identical, model has emerged from the extensive research of Daniel Goleman that resulted in his framework of Emotional Intelligence **(EI)** (Goleman 1998). Again, most of this research was done in the USA. Professor Beverly Alimo-Metcalfe and colleagues at the University of Leeds **(AM&)** have conducted illuminating research on leadership in the UK public sector and have proposed modifications to the mainline Transformational Leadership model to bring it more in line with the culture of British organizations such as the NHS (Alimo-Metcalfe and Alban-Metcalfe 2005a). Further, the Hay Group **(HAY)** was commissioned in 2000 by the former NHS Leadership Centre to research and develop a leadership model for NHS chief executives and directors. At the edge of leadership thinking are such concepts as 'self-organizing effort' from the study of group-as-leader and complex adaptive systems (Plsek and Greenhalgh 2001; Plsek and Wilson 2001) **(EDGE).**

Based on a review of the main source areas cited in the preceding paragraph, numerous derivative works, including the writings of individuals identified by top leaders in the NHS as 'leading thinkers' on the topic of leadership, and a review of the curricula for leadership development programmes in the USA and the UK, we developed the list of items below. We strongly weighted items from British studies over American works and favoured items based on research over those merely expressing opinion. Citations in parentheses are keyed to the codes in bold above and indicate the evidence base behind each item. Citations are given where there is strong and direct support for the item in that source. Lack of citation should not be interpreted as counter-evidence; none of the items in the list below is counter-indicated by evidence from other sources.

The successful leader

- communicates clear (shared) vision, direction, and roles (AM&, HAY, TL, EDGE);
- strategically influences and engages others (AM&, HAY, TL, EI, EDGE)
- builds relationships and works collaboratively with individuals, within teams and across organizational boundaries;
- challenges thinking and encourages flexibility, creativity and innovation (AM&, HAY, TL, EI, EDGE);
- drives for results and improvement (AM&, HAY, EI);
- practises political astuteness (AM&, HAY);
- displays self-awareness and emotional intelligence (AM&, HAY, EI);
- manages personal and organizational power and values diversity (AM&, HAY);
- nurtures a culture in which leadership can be developed and enabled in others (AM&, HAY, TL, EI, EDGE);
- ethically manages self, people and resources;
- commits with passion to values and mission (AM&, HAY, TL);
- demonstrates mastery of management skills (AM&, HAY, TL).

These items are further described in Box 7.2 (see p. 161) and are listed in Figure 7.2. (see p. 158)

Domain: Improvement Knowledge and Skills refers to the disciplines of quality assurance and improvement of both health and health care, which includes such things as process analysis, design, measurement, customer needs research, and so on.

How does the domain of Improvement Knowledge and Skills – *the study and practice of enhancing the performance of process and systems of work* – inform our efforts in the LHIP to develop exceptional leaders of health improvement?

Brief synopsis of the research findings

Improvement science was born in the 1920s in manufacturing and because of these roots it is a pragmatic science. There are, however, few well-designed research studies. The strong evidence for the effectiveness of its various concepts is largely case report and expert opinion. Therefore, we reviewed numerous case reports, carried out a content analysis of compilations of expert views, and conducted opinion leader research in the NHS. Opinion leader research identified Professor Donald Berwick, Institute of Healthcare Improvement, IHI, USA as one of the most respected thinkers on this topic **(IHI)**. Improvement science has been adapted to the NHS through the work, publications, and educational materials that we reviewed from leading organizations such as the Faculty of Public Health **(FPH)**, Royal College of General Practitioners, NHS Modernization Agency, and others (NHS Modernization Agency 2004; NHS Leadership Centre 2003) **(UK)**. The evolution of improvement science includes numerous efforts at repackaging the basic concepts with a new emphasis and terminology **(EVOL)**; for example, Re-engineering, Lean Thinking and Six Sigma. Whilst there is certainly a 'fad' mentality accompanying these various incarnations, there are certain concepts and methods that can be identified as more durable and reliably useful across the fads. We see these as forming the core of improvement science. Unique to health and social care is the broad topic of patient- or client-centred care **(PCC)**. Whilst this draws on the sub-field of customer satisfaction within the improvement sciences, it is important to acknowledge that in many ways patients, clients, carers and the community are more than the typical 'customer'. When applying these concepts to public health, and more generally to health improvement then a more holistic community approach to improvement, is required than would typically apply in the provision of 'health care'.

Based on a review of numerous materials from the four broad source areas above, we developed the list of items below. We sought mainly items that represent consensus among leading thinkers, NHS experience, Faculty of Public Health core competencies, and core concepts that have endured beyond fads such as the focus on community development as a key public health skill. Citations in parentheses are keyed to the codes in bold above and indicate the evidence base behind each item. Again, lack of citation should not be interpreted as counter-evidence. We seek throughout this programme to include models and experience of other sectors, in particular local government, implementing improvement methodologies. We are well aware that the current set of public health competencies is not exhaustive and that many important dimensions are not included. We are also aware of the importance of concepts like 'power' and 'influence' and we intend to address these in the LHIP.

The successful improvement leader
- sees whole systems and any counter-intuitive linkages within them (UK, IHI, EVOL);

- brings in the experiences and voice of the communities and staff (UK, IHI, PCC);
- seeks to create new evidence and translate it into practice (UK, IHI, FPH);
- exposes processes to mapping, analysis and redesign (UK, IHI, EVOL, PCC);
- encourages flexible, innovative rethinking of processes and systems (UK, IHI, EVOL);
- sets up measurement to demonstrate impact and gain insight into variation (UK, IHI, EVOL);
- facilitates reflective practice (UK, IHI, EVOL);
- develops quality and risk management within an evaluation risk culture (FPH);
- works constructively with the human dimension (psychology) of change (UK, IHI);
- sustains and embeds past improvement and drives for continuous improvement (UK, IHI);
- spreads improvement ideas and knowledge widely and quickly (UK, IHI).

These items are further described in Box 7.3 (see p. 164) and are listed in Figure 7.2 (see p. 158).

Domain: Health Improvement Systems – *the practical realities and future possibilities of how interconnected health improvement is experienced by staff and communities.* How do they inform our efforts in the LHIP to develop exceptional leaders for health improvement?

Strengthening the health improvement system means that organizations are better placed to focus on addressing the health needs of their whole populations, including those people in need of NHS treatment or care. Through a system-wide approach to focusing on people and communities, a health improvement system orientation empowers individual organizations to address health inequalities within their populations. Health improvement is key to ensuring that local people have access to effective health promoting, preventive and health protection interventions, as well as to the highest quality clinical services, based upon objective assessment of the needs of the population being served, and evidence of the effectiveness of any planned services.

It is important that health improvement considerations are applied to all decision-making in order to achieve national targets, including Public Service Agreement targets and the implementation of National Service Frameworks. This is why all front-line staff in a range of organizations need an awareness of the main determinants of health and ill health – although advised by specialists, public health must be everyone's business. This includes the three domains of public health identified by the Faculty: health protection, health promotion, and health development, with a concern for reducing health inequalities acting as a cross-cutting theme in respect of all three domains.

Brief synopsis of the research findings

Obviously, health improvement is a dynamic and ever-changing topic. The research in this domain initially focused on interviews with identified leading thinkers and builds on the competencies identified by the Faculty of Public Health (currently being updated) and, as we progress, by LHIP participants themselves.

It is important to note that we make no claim to universality in describing the successful health improvement system. Similar to the items in the leadership domain, but to an even greater degree, we are describing the key elements of the successful health improvement system in the context of England. As we move to an even greater focus on partnership working, shared resources and new roles, Local Area Agreements seem likely to be a powerful driver of future delivery and is consistent with thinking by the Local Government Association, NHS Confederation, and others.

Successful health improvement systems

■ promote and protect the population's health and well-being;

■ develop health programmes and services and reduce inequalities;

■ proactively build on surveillance and assessment of the population's health and well-being;

■ encourage and implement evidence-based practice;

■ operationalize a strategic vision of the future – encompassing trends in society, technology, funding and the workforce;

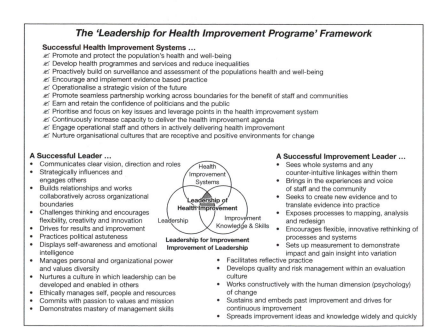

Figure 7.2 *The Leadership for Health Improvement Programme framework*

- promote seamless partnership working across boundaries for the benefit of communities and staff;
- earn and retain the confidence of the politicians and the public;
- prioritize and focus on the key issues and leverage points in the health improvement system;
- continuously increase capacity to deliver the health improvement agenda by improving effectiveness and efficiency and through training and development;
- engage operational staff and others in actively delivering health improvement;
- nurture organizational cultures that are receptive and positive environments for change.

These items are further described in Box 7.4 (see p. 168) and are listed in Figure 7.2.

The modular structure of the LHIP is shown in Figure 7.3.

Interim Evaluation

The external evaluation being conducted by Northumbria University aims to analyse and inform ongoing development of the theory and practice of leadership for health improvement. The study draws on appreciative inquiry and illuminative evaluation methodologies, with objectives to:

- investigate the learning experiences of the programme participants and the participant community through observation, questionnaire and interview data;

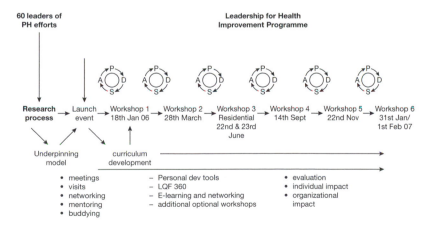

Figure 7.3 *Collaborative model for delivery of the Leadership for Health Improvement Programme based on the Institute of Healthcare Improvement collaborative breakthrough model*

■ explore the process of using this learning in the participant work environment to lead health improvement practices through the analysis of case studies.

Self-evaluation is a built-in component of the programme, but the evaluation also seeks to capture the impact of the programme beyond the individual.

Feedback from participants as the programme enters its second half has been generally positive. Clear messages coming through the interim evaluation as well as from the self-completed evaluation forms following each module show unequivocally that for most participants the programme is meeting a need that has not otherwise been addressed and that the experiences offered and tools and techniques explored are helping equip participants with new perspectives and skills. The networking and relationship building are proving to be a key element to progressing individuals' development. A problem is the limited time available to each module and the difficulty of people creating additional time to pursue issues in greater depth outside the formal meetings.

Conclusions

The LHIP seeks to offer an evidence-based framework of skills and knowledge that, if fully developed, will go far in placing an individual on the road to becoming an exceptional health improvement leader.

The desire to base the LHIP on evidence does not have to mean that it must therefore be 'traditional'. Many of the elements in the proposed framework provide substantial opportunity to stimulate innovative thinking. Indeed, we find strong evidence in all three domains that innovation is key to each domain. By emphasizing mental processes such as challenging, flexible thinking, and purposeful rethinking, we can use a somewhat stable development framework to help participants nevertheless constructively destabilize the health improvement system they wish to modernize and improve.

The list of elements in each individual domain should not be surprising. What is unique about the LHIP is the emphasis on the *whole system* of knowledge, partnership working, and the synergies and overlaps among the domains, and in particular the multi-agency cohort of participants learning and developing together. What we hope will emerge at the end of the programme is a cadre of individuals who will become top-flight leaders of public health, improvers, leaders of improvement, and improvers of their own leadership.

Building on the experience of the NHS Leading Modernization Programme, we know of no other programmes that have pulled together such a foundational evidence base, allow such broad space for innovation, and seek such a complex developmental outcome for participants. Certainly no other programme is aimed at those leading and managing in public health.

BOX 7.2   THE LEADERSHIP DOMAIN

The successful leader

Communicates clear (shared) vision, direction, and roles
(AM&, HAY, TL, EDGE)

The successful leader is clear in his or her own mind about where the organization needs to go, and is able to communicate that message with both credibility and compelling clarity to diverse groups, including the public. This vision is firmly based on shared core values such as patient/community centredness. The leader varies the details of the message depending upon the audience, based on a deep understanding of what is important to various groups and individuals. This leader understands that being inclusive, almost to a fault, in the process of forming a message is a major part of the communication process; that is, good communication is a two-way process where active listening is just as important as clear speaking. Finally, the successful leader realizes that individuals within an organization are being constantly bombarded with messages about many different topics. To ensure clarity, the successful leader 'over communicates', utilizing multiple means to repeatedly get the message out. In terms of addressing the health improvement system, developing shared vision through partnership working is an essential leadership style.

Strategically influences and engages others
(AM&, HAY, TL, EI, EDGE)

The successful leader understands that engaging others in action is the essence of meaningful leadership. The leader also knows that individuals can have their own unique reasons for why they will or will not engage in action, and it is essential to understand these individual rationales. At the same time, this leader is strategic and understands that everyone is not necessarily equal when it comes to the impact of their actions. The successful leader works hard to understand who are the true 'opinion leaders' and 'power brokers' on a given topic and within a given social system. These local leaders (who may not necessarily be in formal roles) are able to lead others, and the successful leader understands that time and effort spent working with them has a multiplying effect.

Builds relationships and works collaboratively with individuals,
within teams and across organizational boundaries
(AM&, HAY, EI, EDGE)

Cultivating relationships is key to getting things done through others. The leader sees relationships everywhere and at the heart of nearly every issue.

161

Generative relationships set the stage for innovative and productive action. The successful leaders work diligently to build constructive relationships at all levels of his or her interaction – one-to-one, within teams, across teams, across major organizational boundaries, and with stakeholders outside the organization. The highly skilled leader is also able to flex his or her style as needed to support relationships. Further, this leader can help mend damaged relationships and can be a skilful diplomat or negotiator when the situation calls for it; but it is also clear that he or she will not allow a bad relationship or power struggle to stop all action.

Challenges thinking and encourages flexibility, creativity and innovation (AM&, HAY, TL, EI, EDGE)

The successful leader makes you think. He or she is constructively provocative, and is comfortable with ambiguity and seeming paradox. This leader looks at either-or choices and asks why it cannot be both-and. He or she is always asking delightfully troubling questions such as Why?, Who says it has to be that way? and Can you think of another way? The leader has a positive outlook, a can-do spirit, and a fundamental belief that answers lie within oneself. While certainly not foolish, this leader is willing to take a risk and try new things. Further, this leader evokes and encourages a similar outlook, spirit and belief from those around him or her. If this leader has a fault it is that of little tolerance for whinging and responses such as 'We've always done it that way'.

Drives for results and improvement (AM&, HAY, EI)

While visioning, relationship building, and developing others are what the leader does, the successful leader realizes that none of that matters if it does not contribute to real organizational results. This leader is clear that the measure of success is accomplishment of the mission and service to stakeholders. While the leader is driven and not afraid to say *what* needs to be accomplished, he or she is also careful to avoid dictating *how* it is to be accomplished. Furthermore, whilst this leader is eager to celebrate success enthusiastically and reward those who contributed, he or she is also continually asking 'How can we now make it even better?' When it comes to results, change is the thing that this leader wants to remain a constant.

Practises political astuteness (AM&, HAY)

The highly skilled leader is well aware that he or she acts within a social and political context made up of other leaders and people of power. These political forces operate both locally and nationally. The successful leader has a keen sense of who needs to be involved in decision-making; who needs to be 'kept on board'; when is the best time to move on an issue; and when it is best not to fight a particular battle. This leader is tuned-in to the political context, but always acts with personal integrity – eschewing gossip, innuendo, and backbiting.

Displays self-awareness and emotional intelligence (AM&, HAY, EI)
What leaders do and how they do it impacts on the lives of many others. The successful leader realizes this and feels a deep sense of personal obligation to understand his or her effect on others. The leader, therefore, seeks feedback (from those above, below, and at peer level in the organizational hierarchy, both within and outside the organization) and reflects deeply, responsibly, and non-defensively about it. This leader knows his or her strengths, challenges shortcomings, triggers, and charms. Consequently, he or she is not easily misled, is approachable, is confident without being arrogant, and is tolerant and forgiving towards others. Such leaders are comfortable in their own skin and comfortable to be around.

Manages personal and organizational power and values diversity
(AM&, HAY)
There exists an ambivalence about power and its importance for influencing behaviour and getting people to do things they would not otherwise do (Lukes 2005). Critical though it is for effective managerial behaviour, 'power' is often regarded as a dirty word. As Pfeffer notes, 'it is as if we know that power and politics exist, and we even grudgingly admit that they are necessary to individual success, but we nevertheless don't like them' (Pfeffer 1992: 15). The concepts of power and organizational politics are related, with organizational politics being defined as the exercise or use of power (Pfeffer 1992). Learning how to manage with power is regarded as essential to getting things done in organizations and to ensuring successful implementation. Yet training in its use is far from widespread.

Nurtures a culture in which leadership can be developed and enabled in others (AM&, HAY, TL, EI, EDGE)
The true leader sees such grand visions of change, such that there is no way that he or she can do it all alone. Developing, enabling and encouraging others is not just a management duty or something nice to do, it is essential to accomplishing what the leader sees needs to be done. Therefore, this leader spends the greatest portion of his or her time helping others find meaning in their work, providing resources, removing barriers, creating 'air cover' and space for trying new things, coaching, helping others develop their skills, celebrating sincere efforts, and allowing people to make mistakes as long as

163

it leads to learning. When this leader is asked to cite his or her most important career accomplishments, the talk quickly turns to listing the individuals who this leader has watched go on to bigger and better things.

Ethically manages self, people and resources

If leadership is as much about the 'how' as the 'what', then managing ethically is of critical importance. Being seen to 'practice what one preaches' and to be acting fairly at all times has to lie at the heart of leadership and management practice. The process demands being accountable and transparent.

Commits with passion to values and mission (AM&, HAY, TL)

Many might use the word 'passionate' to describe this leader. Such leaders will not compromise on fundamental values such as equity or patient-centredness. Neither will they 'let go' of issues that are crucial to accomplishing the organization's mission. He or she is able to 'feel the fear, but do it anyway', because it is right and needed. This leader has courage, strength, and tenacity; balanced with humility and a sense of service to others. He or she might try a different tack and would certainly be open to input from others, but no one questions where this leader stands and where his or her heart lies.

Demonstrates mastery of management skills (AM&, HAY, TL)

Some would draw a sharp distinction between management and leadership. Clearly, the other items in this framework imply that leadership does go beyond 'good management'. At the same time, a leader cannot reach the levels implied here if he or she cannot skilfully prioritize, project-manage, time-manage, delegate, establish and hold others constructively accountable, grasp issues of finance, and supervise the work of direct reports without meddling and micro managing.

BOX 7.3   THE IMPROVEMENT KNOWLEDGE AND SKILLS DOMAIN

The successful improvement leader

Sees whole systems and any counter-intuitive linkages within them (UK, IHI, EVOL)

The successful improvement leader is a systems-thinker. He or she under-stands that most meaningful outcomes of an organization are the products of interacting structures, processes and patterns. These meaningful 'whole systems' often display complex, non-linear, and sometimes surprising behaviour. The skilled leader is keenly aware that failure to see and involve the whole system when making change can lead to 'unintended consequences' and 'fixes that fail'. Further, they know that people and organizational systems adapt and change over time, for better or for worse, in response to other changes within the system – organizations and the people in them are not machines. Despite these whole-systems issues, the successful improvement leader recognizes the practical need to work with processes, 'chunks,' and partial sub-systems. This leader simply does so by working with ever-larger pieces and avoiding naivety.

Brings in the experiences and voice of the communities and staff
(UK, IHI, PCC)
The successful improvement leader recognizes that the ultimate judge of the quality of a service is the customer. This being the case, it is intuitively obvious to this individual that one of the very first steps in any improvement effort must be a deep understanding of the customer's experience (both for individuals and communities) in interacting with those attempting to improve the system. Since improvement requires change, the improver also realizes that another key set of 'customers' are the staff from a broad range of organizations that must take part in change. The successful leader is constantly seeking innovative and systematic ways to bring the voices of all these 'customers' into the process of improvement.

Seeks to create new evidence and to translate it into practice
(UK, IHI, FPH)
Knowledge of what works and does not work is key to making processes and systems better. 'Evidence' about this comes in a variety of forms – formal studies, case reports, practical experience, the views of experts, and reasonable inferences based on sound theory or models. The successful improvement leader constantly asks: 'How do we know that works?' and is as likely to ask this about the status quo as about a proposed change. The goal in the improver's eye is constantly to narrow the gap between what we *know* and what we *do* in our processes and systems. At the same time, this leader profoundly appreciates 'context' and therefore realizes that the approach to change must necessarily involve local translation and adaptation of knowledge to fit the circumstances, rather than simply copying what worked elsewhere.

165

Exposes processes to mapping, analysis and redesign
(UK, IHI, EVOL, PCC)
While all work is a process and all outcomes are the results of interacting systems, these processes and systems typically lie below the conscious attention of those who work within them. Because people and systems are constantly adapting to changing conditions, even carefully designed processes can, over time, diverge widely from their original state. The successful improvement leader knows that one of the most powerful tools he or she possesses is that which maps process flows to make them concrete and visible in order that their reasonableness can be questioned. The insights gained in this effort can then lead naturally to ideas for change and deliberate redesign.

Encourages flexible, innovative rethinking of processes and systems
(UK, IHI, EVOL)
'There is always a better way' is the mantra of the improver. He or she is playfully restless, constructively provocative, unafraid to take a risk, and unusually free-thinking with regard to organizational processes and systems. Furthermore, this leader utilizes a variety of semi-structured methods to encourage and induce such liberating thinking in others.

Sets up measurement to demonstrate impact and gain insight into variation (UK, IHI, EVOL)
Related to the desire for evidence and the generally analytical flavour of improvement science, the successful leader demands some objective data and facts to indicate that real improvement has occurred. It is not enough to say, 'It seems better now'. At the same time, this leader accepts the wisdom of the late improvement guru W. Edwards Deming who said that often 'the most important things are unknown and unknowable'. Therefore, this leader seeks clever surrogate measures and is comfortable combining objective and subjective assessments of progress. As noted above, the improvement leader is also a systems-thinker and, therefore, typically sets up a suite of indicators to capture various views of system performance and to monitor for unintended consequences. The successful improvement leader also understands that repeated measures will naturally display variation. It is critically important to understand the types and sources of variation, and to distinguish real indications of change from mere random variation.

Facilitates reflective practice (UK, IHI, EVOL)
The successful improvement leader sees himself or herself as a guide or coach in service to others. In the end, they realize that his or her brilliant insight is of limited practical value because he or she is really powerless to bring

about lasting change in an organizational process or system. Only those who actually do the work can really change the work and make it last. Therefore, the improvement leader seeks to master a variety of small- and large-group facilitation and reflective practice techniques with which to guide others to discover their own ideas and insights about what will make things better.

Develops quality and risk management within an evaluation culture (FPH)

It is no longer enough for managers to rely on their experiential knowledge and judgement and to manage by hunch, important though these dimensions of the art of management are. Increasingly, management decisions require to be based as far as possible on evidence of what is effective and why. This demands an evaluation culture in order to reflect upon and learn from previous practice. But what is being proposed here is not a throwback to Taylorism, management science and technical rationality. The phenomena of uncertainty, change and uniqueness are central to the domain of health improvement. The art of managing requires what Schon (1991) terms 'reflection-in-action'. When a manager reflects in action, he draws on his or her stock of knowledge cumulatively built up over time.

Works constructively with the human dimension (psychology) of change (UK, IHI)

All improvement requires change. Nearly all change in human-intensive systems (like health and social care) involves people. The successful improvement leader, while skilled analytically, accepts that people are both rational and emotional beings. He or she knows that technically rational changes can fail if the social and emotional aspects of change are not handled well. This is not an unnecessary bother, but rather a fundamental reality of the system. Therefore, the successful improvement leader is genuinely respectful of others, cuts through negativism and demoralization, seeks to understand deeply why people do what they do, and takes upon themselves the responsibility to present change in ways that are both emotionally and rationally appealing to those who must be involved in the change. As indicated in the leadership domain, self-awareness and high emotional intelligence are key.

Sustains and embeds past improvement and drives for continuous improvement (UK, IHI)

Because systems naturally change and adapt over time, the successful leader knows that improvement work in a given area of the organization is never

167

really finished. This leader takes deliberate steps to ensure structures, processes and patterns are in place that will assure that performance does not degrade back to previous levels. Furthermore, this leader is never content with the way things are and also knows that one of the best ways to prevent degradation of performance is to push on to even better levels of performance. However, he or she is also keenly aware that resources are limited and, therefore, improvement effort must be allocated, prioritized, and dynamically balanced across many processes and systems over time.

Spreads improvement ideas and knowledge widely and quickly
(UK, IHI)
The successful improvement leader is a skilful knowledge manager. He or she knows that ideas for improvement that spring up in one area of an organization could be potentially useful to other areas of the organization, or indeed if not carefully planned could potentially destabilize it. At the same time, this leader understands that the spread of improvement knowledge is the result of an adoption process. That is, individuals and groups need to go through a rational and emotional process in which they see their own need, come to believe that an idea from elsewhere might help meet that need, take the opportunity to rethink the idea so that it becomes their own, and go on to take action to put the idea into practice. While this leader feels a sense of urgency about seeing good ideas spread widely, he or she knows that simply cataloguing and distributing descriptions of improvement ideas is naive, and that dictating 'thou shalt' implement this or that practice is short-sighted. The successful leader therefore knows the value of, and methods for collaborative networking, exploring, sharing, and testing of ideas, and promoting 'assisted wheel re-invention'.

BOX 7.4   THE HEALTH IMPROVEMENT SYSTEMS DOMAIN

Successful health improvement systems

Promote and protect the population's health and well-being
Continuing to strengthen integrated health protection programmes, developed with, and owned by a range of partner organizations, will ensure effective use of local resources. The improvement system will maximize its health protection capacity through effective development and use of staff. Playing an active part and taking responsibility for health emergency planning, immunization programmes, infection control for local populations, services

and premises will be greatly enhanced by stronger local partnership working. Joint strategies for health protection, developed with the Health Protection Agency and other relevant agencies, based on agreed national standards, are critical to local success.

Develop health programmes and services, and reduce inequalities
Identifying priority areas for high impact to address health improvement and health inequalities will have much greater effect if tackled in a structured programmatic approach, using all the resources available through multi-agency partnerships. Joint working on initiatives, including health protection, where there are opportunities for health improvement and reducing inequalities (e.g. tuberculosis, HIV, sexually transmitted infections) will be of much greater impact. Other areas such as safety, crime and disorder, alcohol consumption, etc. will be tackled far more effectively if we can bring the 'right' people to the discussion and planning table, working closely with a wide range of partner organizations, including the police, fire service, education, etc.

Proactively build on surveillance and assessment of the population's health and well-being
Staff from a wide range of organizations, through local Strategic Partnerships and Local Area Agreements, are beginning to work together on decreasing health inequalities and improving health and well-being at a local level. In order to strengthen these partnerships we need to increase capability for surveillance and assessment using basic tools such as community profiling, risk assessment and health impact assessments – through to sophisticated methodologies and databases developed by the Public Health Observatories. Sharing, building on and implementing the knowledge being developed will lead to far greater evidence for measurement of improvement and for attracting resources.

Encourage and implement evidence-based practice
With the increased availability of a wide range of data from different organizations, it is important that staff have access to such information, including research and evidence reviews. However having access to the information does not mean that it will be put into practice, and systems need to be in place for monitoring the uptake and implementation of such evidence. Increasing skills to interpret and implement evidence-based practice, including capabilities in relation to the collation, appraisal and evaluation of the evidence, is essential.

Operationalise a strategic vision of the future – encompassing trends in society, technology, funding, and the workforce
Successful organizations create and maintain a mid- to long-term vision of where they are going. They are constantly looking for new possibilities that fit with their values and help further the accomplishment of their mission. This vision of the future is continuously and systematically informed by social trends that shape the wants and needs of stakeholders; technological advances that create new possibilities (medical technology, information technology, new concepts in service provisioning, new ways of collecting and collating data, etc.); funding streams that enable or block innovation; and the desires and capabilities inherent in the people that the organization relies on to actually do the work. However, such vision is mere words without strategies, plans and actions that help realize it. While successful organizations do their share of short-term problem-solving and reaction to issues, they keep their eye on the future and steadfastly refuse to let all their resources be consumed by the problems of today.

Promote seamless partnership working across boundaries for the benefit of communities and staff
Nature tells us that boundaries are essential to complex system functioning (imagine what your body would be like if there were not individual cells with walls that allow nutrients to pass through, while blocking or expelling toxic chemicals). Similarly, learning how to work productively across boundaries is essential for a well-functioning care delivery system. Simply reorganizing when the system is not functioning well only creates different boundaries and has a weakening and negative effect on the whole organization (Wanless 2004). If we have not learned to work effectively across the old boundaries, what makes us believe that we will be able to do so with these new ones? Successful health improvement systems demand that power and resources are focused on what is best for those being served, rather than on what is best for my patch, my sub-set of the organization, or my profession. Furthermore, this desire for seamless working, built on developing relationships across boundaries, extends beyond the confines of what is traditionally viewed as health and social care, and reaches out to other public and private sector partners.

Earn and retain the confidence of politicians and the public
Health improvement requires resources. In a publicly funded system the majority of those resources come from taxpayers, by way of their elected representatives. Assuring a continuing stream of resources requires constant

attention to shaping and satisfying the needs and wants of those who provide the funding. Stated this way, the challenge is the same for health and social care systems the world over; it is simply that the identities of the funders may be different. When those who pay the bills lose confidence in an organization's ability or desire to meet their needs and wants, they demand change and often force it by taking their resources elsewhere. Stated this way, the challenge is the same for any organization, in any industry, whether in the public or private sectors, the world over. Earning and retaining the confidence of those who pay the bills is a fundamental requirement for the survival of any organization.

Prioritize and focus on key issues and leverage points in the health improvement system

Resources to meet the developmental needs of a health improvement system are not infinite. Successful organizations, therefore, reflectively examine the interconnections and knock-on effects within their systems to seek leverage points (where focused investments produce widely felt benefits). The leaders of these successful organizations realize that no individual or small group could possibly know all the interconnections and potential knock-on effects, and so they put processes In place to engage a wide array of stakeholders in helping to set these developmental priorities. They demand, however, that these stakeholders go beyond mere advocacy for their part of the system to present a coherent case for how development in one area will benefit many.

Continuously increase capacity to deliver the health improvement agenda

'To serve' is a key mission of a health 'improvement' system. Continuously increasing its capacity to serve and improve is the natural pursuit of the system. Capacity can of course be increased by supplying more and more resources; for example, building more facilities or employing more staff. Successful health improvement systems thoughtfully consider such investments and have deliberate planning processes to direct them. In addition, successful organizations realize the folly associated with employing more staff to do things that are ineffective, or throwing more resources at sub-systems that already waste a large percentage of the resources they have through inefficiency or poor quality. They see reducing ineffectiveness, inefficiency, and waste as an important path to doing more with the resources they have. Appropriate training, skilling-up and new ways of working are important parts of this process.

Engage operational staff and others in actively delivering health improvement

Because of fundamental values regarding respect for professional judgement, professional groups actually control most of the resource use and process flows in a care delivery system. Actively engaging those at the 'sharp end' of care in the pursuit of increasing the capacity to prevent and promote health improvement is therefore essential to the success of any health or social care system. Change will not happen, or if it does happen will not be enduring, without engaging the hearts and minds of those who actually provide the delivery point of the service. An example of this might be that if we want to reduce the number of admissions to hospital then we need to engage and work with a whole host of agencies other than health, but it would be wholly unproductive to do this without the inclusion of the clinicians in both secondary and primary care.

Nurture organizational cultures that are receptive and positive environments for change

Evolving into the future with more equity, better health protection and stronger emphasis on health promotion requires change. Organizations where the conversation is predominately about what we cannot or will not change, or about who is to blame for what is currently lacking, are greatly impeded on their journey into the future. Successful organizations see change as invigorating, helpful, and possible. While there will always be pessimists, successful health improvement systems cultivate enough positive thinking among leaders and staff to create the momentum needed to move them into their future.

DISCUSSION QUESTIONS

1 Do you consider the approach and content of the Leadership for Health Improvement Programme to be appropriate for public health leaders and managers?

2 Do you think the approach has limitations and, if so, how might they be overcome?

3 What are the constraints to introducing such a programme more widely?

4 What measures might be identified to demonstrate the success of such a programme?

REFERENCES

Alimo-Metcalfe, B. and Alban-Metcalfe, J. (2005a) Leadership: time for a new direction? *Leadership*, 1(1): 51–71.

Alimo-Metcalfe, B. and Alban-Metcalfe, J. (2005b) The crucial role of leadership in meeting the challenges of change. *VISION – The Journal of Business Perspective*, 9(2): 27–39.

Goleman, D. (1998) *Working with emotional intelligence*. London: Bloomsbury.

Lukes, S. (2005) *Power: a radical view*. 2nd edition. Basingstoke: Palgrave.

NHS Leadership Centre (2003) *NHS leadership qualities framework*. London: Department of Health.

NHS Modernization Agency (2004) *NHS leadership qualities*. London: Department of Health.

Nutbeam, D. and Wise, M. (2002) Structures and strategies for public health intervention, in R. Detels, J. McEwen, R. Beaglehole and H. Tanaka (eds) *Oxford textbook of public health. The practice of public health*, Volume 3, 4th edition. Oxford: Oxford University Press, pp. 1873–1888.

Pfeffer, J. (1992) *Managing with power: politics and influence in organisations*. Cambridge, Mass.: Harvard Business School Press.

Plsek, P.E. and Greenhalgh, T. (2001) The challenge of complexity in health care. *British Medical Journal*, 323: 625–628.

Plsek, P. and Wilson, T. (2001) Complexity leadership, and management in healthcare organisations. *British Medical Journal*, 323: 746–749.

Rao, M. (2006) Developing public health leadership. *ph.com*, June: 12.

Schon, D.A. (1991) *The reflective practitioner: how professionals think in action*. Aldershot: Avebury.

Wanless, D. (2004) *Securing good health for the whole population*. Final report. London: HM Treasury.

World Health Organization (WHO) (1998) *Strengthening public health*. Copenhagen: WHO.

Chapter 8

Conclusion

David J. Hunter

There can be few more challenging management tasks in any human organization than that arising from improving the public's health. This is particularly so at a time of continuous policy and organizational change. Yet, paradoxically, despite its complexity and importance, the management role of those engaged in public health has received minimal attention until very recently. A recurring theme of this book has been the importance of the management role to public health. As Derek Wanless stated in his report on the state of public health:

> A step change will be required to move us on to a fully engaged path. In practice full engagement will mean achieving the best outcomes that individuals in aggregate are willing to achieve with strong leadership and sound organisation of all the many efforts being made to help them.
>
> (Wanless 2004: 10)

As earlier chapters have shown, promoting healthier communities and tackling health inequalities are challenges that can only be met locally by working in partnerships. Multi-agency partnerships are non-hierarchical and require leadership and management without authority and often through ambiguity. Such partnerships can be fragile and require developing a high regard for emotional intelligence, leading to greater awareness of self and others. But the necessary partnerships are not simply those occurring across organizations but also those within them. For example, within the NHS engaging, involving and developing clinicians as public health leaders and champions is essential for progress to be made, since the NHS has tended to neglect prevention in favour of crisis intervention and acute care.

The book has endeavoured to bring together analysis of policy and practice with an exploration of their implications for management and leadership for health, and what this suggests by way of appropriate models for conducting these functions and preparing and equipping those who undertake them with the appropriate skills and competences. The combination is essential since management and leadership are ultimately contextual. It is a serious mistake to underplay or ignore the environmental, economic, political and social influences that invariably shape, and impact on, managerial performance (Blackler 2006; Goodwin 2006). A good example of the interaction comes from a former senior policy adviser to the British prime minister who, after leaving government and becoming a school teacher in South London, reflected on the marked contrast between the two settings:

> Perhaps the biggest eye-opener for me on my journey has been how the approach I had been part of creating, to deal with the 24 hour media and to demonstrate a decisive government, was entirely the wrong one for convincing frontline professionals, or indeed for ensuring effective delivery. Our approach to political strategy had been based on three things: momentum, conflict and novelty, whereas the frontline requires empowerment, partnership and consistency.
>
> (Hyman 2005: 384)

A policy environment that can often be confused and incoherent inevitably makes the managerial and leadership challenges more difficult. It is generally accepted that the health policy field constitutes such an environment. In their study of incentives for managers to focus on wider health issues in England, Hunter and Marks (2005: 50) concluded that 'what is needed to encourage management for health is a consistent message, backed by sustained political commitment and leadership at the highest level'. They stress that although this is not a new message, it bears repeating because it seems to have little impact – a conclusion shared by the Chief Medical Officer for England himself in his 2005 annual report. As he observes,

> this situation has not been created by any person or group of people. It is the result of many disparate factors, but at its heart is a set of attitudes that emphasises short-term thinking, holds too dear the idea of the hospital bed and regards the prevention of premature death, disease and disability as an option not a duty.
>
> (Department of Health 2006: 44)

Against such a policy background it is little wonder, then, that managers in health and other public services in the UK have had very little scope to do more than impose government priorities on their organization and communities even where they know these are likely to be ineffective or have perverse consequences. Despite the admirable rhetoric and policy outpourings affirming the government's commitment to public health, and moving away from the preoccupation with acute health care and hospital beds, the stark reality remains one where the precise opposite persists with public health being marginalized, as acknowledged by the CMO for England (Department of Health 2006).

175

This, then, has been the context for the management and leadership issues discussed in this book, and although the context has primarily been a UK one it seems unlikely that the situation is so different elsewhere in Europe or in countries further afield. Indeed, it is likely that the differences will be ones of degree or emphasis rather than of substance. We have also noted important evolving differences within the UK since political devolution in 1999 and the creation of new governmental institutions in Scotland and Wales.

Moving on from the governmental and political context shaping health policy, previous chapters have taken the concept of public health management in order to begin to fashion a different approach to tackling the challenge of health improvement and to do so in a way that moves away from the flawed, top-down, mechanistic approach based on New Public Management principles that has characterized the target culture in public services.

Managing and leading for health is perhaps best pursued through viewing health improvement as a complex adaptive system. Public services have more in common with such systems than with machines (Chapman 2004; Caulkin 2004; Seddon 2003). Almost by definition, and with few exceptions, public health issues are ones that cannot be controlled or predicted by adopting mechanistic means or principles derived from scientific management thinking.

All this may be unsettling for some managers, especially those trained in a rational, positivist scientific tradition with a stress on linear thinking, because it requires acknowledging that the system they are working in is beyond their control. Nevertheless, as earlier chapters have attempted to demonstrate, it is possible to affect, and to some extent direct, complex adaptive systems. Moreover, such a way of thinking also opens up new ways of thinking about what managing for health entails in terms necessary skills.

The requisite management and leadership skills (and behaviours) that need to be acquired and developed include:

- making best use of available information and data;
- networking and sharing best practice;
- understanding and translating national guidance into local actions;
- making better use of the skills of the public health workforce across a local area in order to do the things that will give the greatest impact.

In addition to a lack of these behavioural skills, there is also an absence of technical skills throughout the public health workforce, including:

- using data and measurement for improvement;
- process redesign;
- storytelling skills;
- tools for creativity and innovation;
- knowledge of social marketing;

- managing the human dimension of change;
- the ability to create social movements and to spread and sustain good practice.

All of these dimensions are reflected in the example of the leadership for health improvement programme described in Chapter 7. Some, like storytelling, may seem unusual to some readers and yet it can be a powerful learning tool for managers and practitioners (Greenhalgh 2006). But, as Greenhalgh points out, narrative approaches to organizational and management studies are seen as 'soft' and marginal rather than central in the prevailing political climate in the UK and perhaps elsewhere, too. As she notes, in keeping with a theme of this book,

> The 'make it happen' mindset of the new public management requires the setting of explicit performance outputs, and depressingly often restricts the focus of both 'quality assurance' and 'research' to establishing the efficiency and cost-effectiveness with which these predefined outputs are achieved.
>
> (Greenhalgh 2006: 59)

The problem is that stories are unpredictable and may contain uncomfortable truths that managers and practitioners may be reluctant to confront. NPM thinking is unsympathetic to such messiness. It feels more comfortable with something that is explicit, controllable and auditable, like a protocol or guideline or target.

What the LHIP has also attempted to demonstrate explicitly is the importance of power and politics in managing for health. Paradoxically, managers are engaged in power plays and immersed in politics (of all types) in their daily lives, although they are often reluctant to admit it or condone such activity as legitimate and important. Some might argue that in the British NHS managers have become too political while, conversely, politicians have become too managerial, and this is a real problem that has arguably reduced managers' effectiveness. Nevertheless, unless power and politics are regarded as legitimate management tools then sustainable change is unlikely to occur. As we have argued in Chapter 1 and elsewhere, despite general agreement that it is more humane and cost-effective to keep people healthy than to have to treat the consequences of not doing so later, modern health systems continue to emphasize curative downstream approaches. A large part of the reason for this is the power of the medical community and allied professional groups who have an intrinsic interest in curative medicine and in maintaining, if not increasing, investment in it. It is a dominant force in all health care systems (Blank and Burau 2004; Department of Health 2006). In contrast to curative medicine, the public have little or no appreciation or understanding of the mission and content of public health. Even in respect of high-profile public health issues like smoking and alcohol, the contribution of public health managers is only dimly perceived if at all. There are sound reasons for this as we have seen in Chapter 2, many of them the result of a

diverse and wide-ranging workforce not all of whose members would regard themselves as public health practitioners. Public health cannot be neatly packaged and organized within a single set of organizational boundaries. It extends across many agencies and groups and levels of government. Hence the appeal of a notion like the public health system. It provides an organizing framework for the rather ill-defined field known as public health.

In its review of public health in the twenty-first century, the Institute of Medicine (IOM) viewed the public health system as the organizational mechanism for achieving the best population health:

> The concept of a public health system describes a complex network of individuals and organisations that have the potential to play critical roles in creating the conditions for health. They can act individually, but when they work together toward a health goal, they act as a system – a public health system.
>
> (IOM 2003: 28)

The core features of a public health system have been considered in Chapter 2, and Griffiths, *et al.* (2005) have summarized them for a UK context as follows:

- a national policy framework;
- a network of public health specialists working at all population levels: local, regional, national, international;
- providing comprehensive public health programmes for populations, including vulnerable groups, to improve and protect health;
- as an integral part of primary care, working with all partners;
- led in each locality/geographic area by a director of public health;
- working through locally organized multidisciplinary public health teams made up of specialists, practitioners, clinicians and interested people in communities, including voluntary and community groups and community advocates, who are all part of managed public health networks.

Irrespective of the precise details of the above list of features, an effective public health system needs a robust infrastructure supported by timely, accurate and accessible public health information and informed by good research evidence. Strong partnerships with communities and a variety of public and private agencies are also essential across the three domains of public health practice.

But however we define public health or the public health system, it will count for little if the managers and leaders populating it are not equipped with the appropriate skills. As we have considered in earlier chapters, there exists a view in some quarters that public health practitioners/managers are essentially 'dreamers', thinking up worthy but unworkable or unrealistic schemes for health gain, while managers are essentially 'pragmatists', with their feet firmly on the ground. Certainly,

some managers view their public health colleagues in such a light, regarding them as lacking the discipline to carry through the necessary processes of hard decision-making. In one study a manager is quoted as saying that 'some public health physicians are perceived to be intellectually time-consuming in terms of discussions about how jolly difficult it all is' (Richardson, et al. 1994:46). A decade or more later, such views can still be heard, although possibly less commonly. However, it seems likely that the desperate state in which public health in England finds itself, judging from the CMO's hard-hitting critique in his annual report for 2005, is evidence of such prejudices remaining alive. It is not simply a matter of structures or numbers of public health practitioners, although these are not unimportant. But perhaps more critical is having a workforce that understands its purpose and has been developed to achieve it. For the most part, as we have seen, there are significant deficits that remain to be addressed. Some of these lie not only within the public health community but in the traditional health care management and clinical domains. More than ever, if health care services are not to become unsustainable as they struggle to cope with rising demand from chronic diseases and a failure to deal with public health problems, managers of all types within health care systems will need to become managers for health and not merely managers for health care or managers of facilities.

Indeed, this was the view of those interviewed for the study cited earlier that sought to identify the incentives and levers that might be used to bring about change towards meeting health policy objectives (Hunter and Marks 2005). They were clear that a proactive approach was the hallmark of a public health organization and would require changes in organizational culture, in the mindset of practitioners as well as system change (Marks and Hunter 2005). A proactive health organization would have the characteristics listed in Box 8.1.

If indeed, as Beaglehole and Bonita assert, 'we are entering a new era in which the public health perspective will become more central to the health development agenda', then we need to move beyond analysis to action with some urgency (Beaglehole and Bonita 2004: 253). And that requires not 'dreamers' but 'pragmatists' and advocates for real change. And that, in turn, requires managers and leaders for whom health improvement is at the core of their mission and purpose. This is difficult and painstaking work for which there are no quick fixes or shortcuts. Indeed, the likelihood of success is hard to gauge and may well defeat even the most talented managers and leaders. Despite the increased attention public health receives today in many countries, expenditure on such efforts represents only a minor aspect compared with spending on curative medical care (Mechanic 2003; Department of Health 2006). The future of public health policy and practice therefore remains fragile and unpredictable. In his assessment of whether or not population health has a future, Mechanic states rather sombrely:

A great deal depends on the political climate, which is difficult to foresee. Some political contexts and political administrations are more prone to

---

BOX 8.1 KEY CHARACTERISTICS OF A PROACTIVE PUBLIC HEALTH ORGANIZATION

- It would have public health at its centre.
- There would be a public health ethos throughout the organization.
- It would intervene as early as possible in the continuum of health and address the issue of potentially avoidable deaths with urgency.
- It would maximize the use of existing preventive initiatives such as breast screening or vaccination for other health improvement activities.
- It would be confident of its long-term agenda.
- There would be commitment from the chief executive and board.
- It would act as a responsible corporate citizen, fulfilling its economic potential to improve health.
- Finance, commissioning, modernization and health improvement strategies would be integrated.
- Primary care organizations would provide data to inform preventive activities in primary care.
- The health improvement agenda would be reflected in workforce development.
- There would be ring fenced resources for public health.

---

social interventions than others. A great deal depends on how issues affecting social determinants are conceptualised and communicated and the astuteness with which representatives of the field convey their understanding.

(Mechanic 2003: 439)

It is hoped that this book has, in a modest way, helped chart a way forward by providing some insights, frameworks and perspectives to assist and guide those who are embarking, or who have already embarked, upon their epic and hazardous journey to improve the public's health. There can be no greater management and leadership challenge in health policy, and no greater reward for making real and sustainable progress.

REFERENCES

Beaglehole, R. and Bonita, R. (2004) Strengthening public health for the new era, in R. Beaglehole (ed.) *Global public health: a new era*. Oxford: Oxford University Press, pp. 253–268.

Blackler, F. (2006) Chief executives and the modernisation of the English National Health Service. *Leadership,* 2(1): 5–30.

Blank, R. and Burau, V. (2004) *Comparative health policy.* Basingstoke: Palgrave Macmillan.

Caulkin, S. (2004) Take aim: you'll always miss. *Observer,* 14 November.

Chapman, J. (2004) *System failure: why governments must learn to think differently,* 2nd edition. London: Demos.

Department of Health (2006) *On the state of the public health: annual report of the chief medical officer 2005.* London: Department of Health.

Goodwin, N. (2006) *Leadership in health care: a European perspective.* London: Routledge.

Greenhalgh, T. (2006) *What seems to be the trouble? Stories in illness and healthcare.* Oxford: Radcliffe Publishing.

Griffiths S, Jewell, T. and Donnelly, P. (2005) Public health in practice: the three domains of public health. *Public Health,* 119: 907–913.

Hunter, D.J. and Marks, L. (2005) *Managing for health: what incentives exist for NHS managers to focus on wider health issues?* London: King's Fund.

Hyman, P. (2005) *1 out of Ten: from Downing Street vision to classroom reality.* London: Vintage.

Institute of Medicine (IOM) (2003) *The future of the public's health in the 21st Century.* Washington: National Academies Press.

Marks, L. and Hunter, D.J. (2005) Moving upstream or muddying the waters? Incentives for managing for health. *Public Health,* 119: 974–980.

Mechanic, D. (2003) Who shall lead: is there a future for population health? *Journal of Health Policy, Politics and Law,* 28(2–3): 421–442.

Richardson, A., Duggan, M. and Hunter, D.J. (1994) *Adapting to new tasks: the role of public health physicians in purchasing health care.* Leeds: Nuffield Institute.

Seddon, J. (2003) *Freedom from command & control: a better way to make the work work.* Buckingham: Vanguard Education.

Wanless, D. (2004) *Securing good health for the whole population.* Final report. London: HM Treasury.

Index